PHALLIC CRITIQUES

Masculinity and Twentieth-Century Literature

Peter Schwenger

Routledge & Kegan Paul
London, Boston, Melbourne and Henley

First published in 1984
by Routledge & Kegan Paul plc

39 Store Street, London WC1E 7DD, England

9 Park Street, Boston, Mass. 02108, USA

464 St Kilda Road, Melbourne,
Victoria 3004, Australia and

Broadway House, Newtown Road,
Henley-on-Thames, Oxon RG9 1EN, England

Set in VIP Palatino, 10 on 12 pt
by Inforum Ltd, Portsmouth
and printed in Great Britain
by St Edmundsbury Press Ltd
Bury St Edmunds, Suffolk

Library of Congress Cataloging in Publication Data

Schwenger, Peter, 1942–

Phallic critiques.
Includes index.
1. Fiction—Men authors—History and criticism.
2. Fiction—20th century—History and criticism.
3. Masculinity (Psychology) in literature. 4. Sex role
in literature.   I. Title.
PN3403.S36 1984   809.3'353   83–24626

British Library CIP data available

ISBN 0-7102-0164-8

to Heinz and Eva Bruhl

CONTENTS

Acknowledgments   ix

Introduction   1

1 The language of men   16

2 Reserve and its reverse   36

3 The cult of the body   51

4 The pen and the penis   71

5 The novel as a dirty joke   82

6 A fabled hunting   97

7 Supermale   118

8 The terrain of truth   133

Afterword   154

Notes   158

Index   169

ACKNOWLEDGMENTS

The poem 'the boys I mean are not refined' on page 19 is reprinted from NO THANKS by E.E. Cummings, by permission of Liveright Publishing Corporation. Copyright © 1935 by E.E. Cummings. Copyright © 1968 by Marion Morehouse Cummings. Copyright © 1973, 1978 by The Trustees for the E.E. Cummings Trust. Copyright © 1973, 1978 by George James Firmage. Reprinted also by permission of Granada Publishing Ltd. The poem 'Down, Wanton, Down!' by Robert Graves on page 76 is reprinted by permission of Robert Graves.

INTRODUCTION

Feminist critics of the last two decades have often expressed their resentment of the so-called 'phallic critics' – men who filter their judgments of women's writing through their own sexist preconceptions. The title of *Phallic Critiques*, then, may seem to promise a backlash, when in fact the book is a natural extension of what feminist literary criticism is doing. We must move beyond protesting phallic biases solely because of their effect on women: it is now imperative to look closely at those biases and to analyse their effect on the men who possess them. In particular, I want to analyse the effect of masculine biases on literature – on writing by men, rather than by women. The chapters that follow are analyses of a certain phallic impulse in twentieth-century literature, and its effect on literary style. If that makes me a phallic critic, so be it; it is probably better than calling myself a 'hominist', a term once suggested by George Bernard Shaw.

This new version of phallic criticism is part of a more general area which has already received much attention from feminist critics: the interface of sexuality and literary style. So at the very outset, this book revives all the questions that have already been raised, though hardly laid to rest. Given the area's complex nature, each question raises another and larger one, so that Alps on Alps arise. I want to consider the question of male and female styles. But this evolves into the question of whether such styles reflect actual differences in male and female perception; and the larger question of whether such differences in fact exist is an enormous and controversial one. Feminists are split on it. For Rosalind Miles the question itself is the thin end of a wedge: 'There is an implicit and inescapable antifeminism in any insistence upon the difference between the sexes.'[1] Patricia Meyer

Spacks, on the other hand, asserts that 'the mind has a sex.' 'How,' she asks, 'can women fail to be in some vital respects – psychic as well as physical – different from men?'[2] If we go ahead and assume the existence of such psychic or perceptual differences, we are faced with the question of how to account for them. Do we ascribe them to nature or to nurture? The two are often confused, as in Erik Erikson's notorious attempt to determine sex differences by comparing the kind of scenes constructed by boys and girls. The fact that so many of the girls constructed enclosed domestic scenes led him to assert the importance of 'inner space' for women – a perceptual construct deeply rooted in their biological construction. However, as Kate Millett has pointed out, the subjects of this experiment were in their teens, well socialized to their sex roles; and 'Erikson's whole theory is built on psychoanalysis' persistent error of mistaking learned behavior for biology.'[3]

If the 'self evident' psychological truth often turns out to be just a product of social conditioning, our hope is that dispassionate research and common sense wil be enough to liberate us. However, even when popular truths are proven erroneous their influence may linger willy-nilly. I once heard a group of intelligent men, feminists all, discuss Mailer's book *The Prisoner of Sex*. They knew that the ideas he advanced there were medical hogwash – such as the notion that the personal qualities of a child reflect the qualities of the act by which it was conceived ('good fucks make good babies'). Still these men had to admit that such ideas exerted a powerful pull on them. And we need not invoke the special privileges of an 'archetype' here. As much as an archetype, its lesser cousins, popular myth and stereotype, may be founded on the erroneous or undesirable. Merely to point this out is not enough to remove all potency; ideas need not be true in order truly to affect us.

The massive problems of sex definition, then, loom behind any analysis of male and female style. In a sense, however, the definition of sex *is* style. Even the most intimate aspects of our lives are influenced by styles of various sorts, encountered at various levels – and this includes the very nature of male and female. Margaret Mead was one of the first to argue (perhaps in too partisan a way) that all cultures set up societal norms for the sexes which go beyond the biological differences. These are so heavily sanctioned that they may appear almost as natural as biology to a particular culture at a particular time. Few people realize that where sexual definition is concerned cultures differ from one another; and, as time passes, these cultures differ from their earlier selves. An example of such a shift within a culture is the English proscription against men crying. In the eighteenth century it was downright fashionable to be a 'Man of Feeling' and to cry publicly at any suitable provocation. But the nineteenth century saw major changes in the idea of masculinity, and among them the rise of the 'stiff upper lip'. Boys' books in particular inculcated this idea increasingly as the century progressed. It was not until the 1880s, though, that the 'stiff upper lip' became a set feature of masculinity.[4] Many of the currently accepted characteristics of masculinity evolve in this way and not out of some innate necessity. They become the prevailing style.

Obviously 'style' here has more to do with fashion than with literary style. Yet the fashion is reflected in literature, and often set by it. Not only does an author present male and female roles, roles which may be viewed as one kind of style; in choosing a literary style he or she presents those roles in a certain tone, a certain accent. The subtle expectations that one has of others and of one's self in this matter of the sexes can be more accurately conveyed by literary style than by an official articulation.

Literary style, then, has an important relation to sexual style; it can be used both to render an existing sex role and to change it. This accounts for the current interest of feminist literary critics like Spacks and Miles in the question of whether all women have to some degree a writing style in common, distinct from that of men. To determine the common characteristics that underlie writing by a wide variety of women would be to learn something about the fundamental qualities of the sex. These qualities, however, need not be seen as fundamental in the sense of unchangeable. So female writers, with no sense of contradicting themselves, are also experimenting with new styles – that is to say, with new ways of giving shape to themselves. While reading the literature of the women's movement, Norman Mailer is struck by its curt sentences, its obscenities, its explosive, aggressive stance. 'A few of the women,' he comments, 'were writing in no way women had ever written before. . . . Some of the women were writing like very tough faggots.'[5] Though backhanded, this is a compliment. 'It was a good style,' he admits – perhaps because it is a style that he himself has often used. It is commonly thought of as a 'masculine' style; and one must consider why women would want to adopt such a style and also why, having adopted it, they should be granted its masculine qualities only as a near miss. This is, however, only one of a number of female styles being experimented with now. And the experiment is hardly the first of its kind.

That women must find new ways of writing is an old theme. One of its most eloquent exponents was Virginia Woolf, with her interest in an elusive entity she called a 'woman's sentence'. Its best practitioner, she found, was Dorothy Richardson:

> She has invented, or, if she has not invented, developed and applied to her own uses, a sentence which we might call the psychological sentence of the feminine gender. It is of a more elastic fibre than the old, capable of stretching to the extreme, of suspending the frailest particles, of enveloping the vaguest shapes. Other writers of the opposite sex have used sentences of this description and stretched them to the extreme. But there is a difference. Miss Richardson has fashioned her sentence consciously, in order that it may descend to the depths and investigate the crannies of Miriam Henderson's consciousness. It is a woman's sentence, but only in the sense that it is used to describe a woman's mind by a writer who is neither proud nor afraid of anything that she may discover in the psychology of her sex.[6]

Woolf may have in mind such a sentence as this, from Richardson's *Pilgrimage*:

> She felt him watching while she waited, gazing through the outspread scene, for words more in harmony than was this arch jocularity with the steady return of the strange new light within her that now streamed forth to join the blinding sunlight, so that she was isolated in a mist of light, far away from him and waiting for the sound of her name.[7]

We can see why Woolf would praise this sinuous psychological sentence; for it has many affinities with Woolf's own type of sentence, especially in the smooth blending of inner and outer worlds. Woolf in fact carries these same characteristics to a greater extreme, and thus provides the best examples of the feminine sentence as she has described it. Here is one from *To the Lighthouse*:

> With some irony in her interrogation, for when one woke at all, one's relations changed, she looked at the steady light, the pitiless, the remorseless, which was so much her, yet so little her, which had her at its beck and call (she woke in the night and saw it bent across their bed, stroking the floor), but for all that she thought, watching it with fascination, hypnotised, as if it were stroking with its silver fingers some sealed vessel in her brain whose bursting would flood her with delight, she had known happiness, exquisite happiness, intense happiness, and it silvered the rough waves a little more brightly, as daylight faded, and the blue went out of the sea and it rolled in waves of pure lemon which curved and swelled and broke upon the beach and the ecstasy burst in her eyes and waves of pure delight raced over the floor of her mind and she felt, It is enough! It is enough![8]

If these women's sentences are being used 'to describe a woman's mind', then what is it that they tell us about that mind? Judging from the work of Woolf and Richardson, we should have to say that the female mind is one of great sensibility; that it is characterized by an intense awareness of detail; that it is aware of nuances of emotion and discriminates finely between them; that it is altogether a mind that puts its trust in the inner life rather than the life of 'telegrams and anger' (in Forster's phrase), the life of action in the world. It has been suggested that numerous other female writers, such as Nathalie Sarraute and Ivy Compton-Burnett, may be characterized in the same way.[9] Perhaps so. But it is worth noting that the qualities just listed, however admirable they may be, are essentially those of the popular stereotype of women. Rosalind Miles's objection to the idea of a feminine style would seem to be borne out here. There are counter-arguments, of course. If the female mind 'naturally' takes this direction, it is likely to be because society stigmatizes any other direction as 'unnatural'. And counter-examples can be found as well. George Eliot is one woman who writes quite differently from Woolf or Richardson. Her style – described by Miles as 'detached, educated, omniscient' – has qualities that are usually thought of as masculine.[10] According to some feminist critics, Eliot demon-strates by her success the fallaciousness of attempts to categorize the female mind. According to others – Woolf among them – she hobbles herself with a masculine sentence that is foreign to the instinctive direction of her genius as a woman writer.

But what is the nature of a 'masculine' sentence? Woolf pro-vides us with only one rather limited example:

> The sentence that was current at the beginning of the
> nineteenth century ran something like this perhaps: 'The
> grandeur of their works was an argument with them, not to
> stop short, but to proceed. They could have no higher
> excitement or satisfaction than in the exercise of their art and
> endless generations of truth and beauty. Success prompts to
> exertion; and habit facilitates success.' That is a man's
> sentence; behind it one can see Johnson, Gibbon and the rest.[11]

It is not necessary to analyse in detail the techniques by which this model male sentence is constructed: its tendency to parallel and antithetical structure; its fondness for abstract vocabulary; its sententious utterances. It is enough to say that both the sen-tence's source and its effect lie in 'the sensation of authority'. The phrase is Mary Ellmann's, and it sums up what she sees as the fundamental underlying characteristic of the masculine style.[12] Of course authority is a traditional prerogative of the male; and it is a prerogative exercised with patriarchal grandeur in the nine-teenth century. But as a masculine sentence this will not do in the twentieth century. Anyone writing with such heavy echoes of Johnson and Gibbon today will merely be thought of as pompous. The style is no longer fashionable, except in such behindhand fields as literary criticism, where pomposity may sometimes pass as coin of the realm. Ellmann would like us to think that authority has gone out of fashion altogether, and with it the whole idea of distinguishing between the sexes by their writing style. Their mutual distrust of the authoritative, she says, 'moves men and women writers closer together now'. The new style for both sexes is characterized by such qualities as 'ironic constraint' or 'deliberate rashness'. However, as Ellmann observes in a foot-note, 'it is perhaps necessary to distinguish between varieties of rashness.'[13] We may find that rashness in a peculiarly male context has quite a different effect from rashness in a female context. Nobody, after all, is accusing Mailer of writing like a 'very tough faggot'. Authority remains as much of a male prerogative as ever. It is only that new forms to express it have evolved, forms more appropriate to the twentieth century; and Woolf's 'masculine' sentence must also be replaced by newer examples.

The question of a masculine mode of writing arises naturally out of the current interest in a feminine mode, and is necessary to a full exploration of that interest. As Annette Kolodny has put it, 'If we insist on discovering something we can clearly label as a "feminine mode," then we are honor-bound, also, to delineate its counterpart, the "masculine mode." '[14] To be sure, Kolodny is suggesting a masculine mode in order to remind us of problems that may be overlooked in any facile idea of the feminine mode. Her statement is then something of a challenge to such classifications. However, it is a challenge that should be taken up. With us already is the social context out of which such an investigation would naturally arise; and it is similar to that which saw the rise of women's studies about fifteen years ago. As a men's movement begins to evolve, an increasing number of books are being published which analyse the nature of masculinity; magazines and newsletters proliferate; conferences are organized.[15] Like the women's movement, which provided both its model and its initial impetus, the men's movement is prone to dissension from within, misunderstanding and ridicule from without. Its course, however, is not likely to parallel that of the women's movement simply because the masculine role which it scrutinizes has configurations peculiar to itself. The most obvious difference is that the men's movement lacks the concrete rallying point of economic discrimination; it must necessarily address itself to the subtler psychological dynamics of the male role. It is here that literature, for several reasons, is liable to be called upon: literature provides experiences which, though artificial, may be the common property of millions; it contains insights which, though unsystematized, are still valid; it provides words for perceptions which, until named, may not even be recognized. The time has come, then, for the question of a masculine mode to be taken seriously. It is a question that has never really been asked before: the assumption was always that we already knew the answer.

To call a writer 'masculine' in the nineteenth century was only a compliment of a rather vague sort. Emerson, in *English Traits*, admires the Elizabethans for the 'masculine force' and 'manly style' of their work. However, the only specific elucidation of these terms comes with his suggestion that in the English language the male principle is the Saxon element, while the Latin element is female. Beyond this, he gives nothing more than a welter of impressions.[16] 'Manliness in art,' according to Walter Pater, has to do with 'tenacity of intuition and of consequent purpose, the spirit of construction as opposed to what is literally incoherent or ready to fall to pieces, and, in opposition to what is hysteric or works at random, the maintenance of a standard.'[17] For Gerard Manley Hopkins, too, 'masterly execution . . . is a kind of male gift, and especially marks off men from women.' Indeed 'the male quality is the creative gift.'[18] For the Victorians, then, the manliness of a work was equated with its moral and artistic virtues. Since virtue itself is etymologically virile, this equation should not surprise us. But the new manliness is writing works much more intimately with the specific configurations of a sexual role. Not abstract virtues but particular gestures of maleness are now the source of an author's masculine style, just as being a gentleman has become less important today than the more blunt and direct goal of 'being a man'.

Blunt and direct it may be now, but the goal of manhood is less directly attainable in the twentieth century than ever. An important shift has taken place in the nature of the masculine role, one that Virginia Woolf may have been the first to notice. In *A Room of One's Own* she observes that 'virility has now become self-conscious.'[19] The reasons for this new self-consciousness are historically complex; most of all, men are reacting to women, and to the pressures of the early Women's Movement.[20] A redefinition of themselves by women always necessitates some kind of readjustment by men: either a redefinition of manhood or else a reassertion of the old definition. No longer is there an assumed understanding about manhood; no longer do comfortable generalities suffice. Awareness must increasingly come down to particulars, and more than that, to complexities and ambivalences. The very fact that the masculine role may be examined *as* a role admits the possibility that it is, to some degree, arbitrary. One may then go further to question the benefits of the role and the price that must be paid for them. Perhaps this kind of questioning was always there in individual men before this century. Now, however, it is increasingly brought into the open. Self-consciousness extends beyond the single self to the whole male sex. Manhood is asserted as always, but never so easily as before.

Self-consciousness is of course a pervasive trait of the twentieth century, but in regard to masculinity it has a particularly disconcerting effect. To be self-conscious is to stand off from the self, to be alienated enough from it to observe its arbitrariness and artifice. Where masculinity is concerned this alienation is more poignant because of the nature of that artificial self which is the masculine role in our time. The role has become that of the 'natural' man. Its particular gestures are increasingly less civilized, revelling in rough edges; fists replace rapiers, blue jeans replace silk breeches, obscenity replaces wit. And this is so for all men regardless of class: 'Male working-class forms seem to symbolize masculinity . . . for men of other social classes as well.'[21] At the same time, then, that their role encourages men to become more 'down to earth', more natural, self-consciousness threatens men with the possibility that the natural man is an artifice. This is a genuine threat; and the way that many men meet it is to insist all the more strenuously on their masculinity. A nineteenth-century man could assume his patriarchy with the ease of one settling into a comfortable armchair. A twentieth-century man may assert the same prerogative, but it is an assertion, not an assumption. It is this difference that Virginia Woolf notices in 1929 while reading a recent novel by a man. Such writers as Kipling and Galsworthy, she feels, exemplify the new self-consciousness of men – one which she feels takes its toll on their writing.

'It is fatal,' Woolf tells us, 'for anyone who writes to think of their sex.'[22] This is an odd pronouncement to get from someone who thought deeply about her sex and whose feminism is an important element in her writing. What Woolf means by it is that writers who are thinking about their sex are not thinking about writing; and writing is such a complex and demanding business that one must come to it with a clear head, free of distractions. More than men, women are likely to be distracted by a consciousness of their sex:

> If we express the historic relation between the sexes in terms of master and slave, it is part of the master's privileges not to

> have to think continuously of the fact that he is the master,
> while the position of the slave carries with it the constant
> reminder of his being a slave. It cannot be overlooked that the
> woman forgets far less often the fact of being a woman than the
> man of being a man.[23]

This general self-consciousness on the part of women acquires
particular pointedness in the woman who writes; to write at all is
to fly in the face of patriarchal expectations of a woman's capacity and her proper sphere. Woolf finds that women's writing
through the centuries is consequently warped away from the
true, the straight line; resistance to bias is itself a kind of bias.
Only when Woolf picks up a novel by a 'new woman' of her own
day does she find the beginnings of a new freedom: this author
'wrote as a woman, but as a woman who has forgotten that she is
a woman, so that her pages were full of that curious sexual
quality which comes only when sex is unconscious of itself.'[24]
This woman's freedom is to a large degree freedom from established writing styles which Woolf sees as essentially male; these
impede the natural movements of a woman's mind. 'The weight,
the pace, the stride of a man's mind are too unlike her own for
her to lift anything substantial from him successfully.'[25] Thus *less*
self-consciousness, paradoxically, will be the result of a consciously forged female style. For once the style is at hand, the
sentences will come instinctively, fitting themselves to the shape
of a woman's thoughts.

   Whether women have in fact attained a style that will free them
from self-consciousness is a good question, but it will not be
pursued here. I am concerned with what may have happened to
men. Male writing styles that were comfortably established in the
preceding century are hardly likely to carry over into this one;
new styles must be newly established. In the masculine style of
her day Woolf detected the first signs of strain. Becoming self-
conscious of their sex, male writers are now labouring under a
disadvantage that was formerly women's alone.

   It is too much, however, to say that *every* male writer will
manifest this condition: his sex may not matter for every man as
much as it does for Kipling. Indeed, certain male writers of
Woolf's time have sensibilities that could be described as 'feminine'. In *Femininity and the Creative Imagination* (New York: Barnes
& Noble, 1973), Lisa Appignanensi deals not with women but

with three such men: Henry James, Robert Musil, and Marcel Proust. The last of these, incidentally, was described by Dorothy Richardson as a 'fellow traveller' along the route she had chosen;[26] and all three of these authors might be the 'other writers of the opposite sex' said by Woolf to be writing the feminine sentence. How true can it be, then, to describe the sentence as feminine? Woolf herself, remember, hedges: 'It is a woman's sentence, but only in the sense that it is used to describe a woman's mind. . . .'

There are two points that should be stressed here. First, Woolf's comment reminds us that any attempt to forge a woman's style or a man's style depends to some degree on content. Style does not happen in a void, but interacts with content and from it acquires significance. Masculine or feminine subject matter, then, will influence the effect of any style. Second, it is obvious that 'feminine' and 'masculine' styles need not be apportioned strictly by sex. I have already noted those men of Woolf's own day who wrote a 'feminine' style. To reverse things, one could cite George Eliot's 'masculine' style; or we could consider the case of 'James Tiptree, Jr'. This is the pen name of one of today's most talented science fiction writers; for a long time there was controversy over the writer's identity, and even sex. Robert Silverberg said this:

> It has been suggested that Tiptree is female, a theory that I find absurd, for there is to me something ineluctably masculine about Tiptree's writing. I don't think the novels of Jane Austen could have been written by a man nor the stories of Ernest Hemingway by a woman, and in the same way I believe that the author of the James Tiptree stories is male.

When Alice B. Sheldon confessed that she was Tiptree, it was for Silverberg

> quite a surprise package; and there I was in print upholding the ineluctable masculinity of 'Tiptree's' writing. Okay: no shame attaches. She fooled me beautifully, along with everyone else, and called into question the entire notion of what is 'masculine' or 'feminine' in fiction. I am still wrestling with that.[27]

Plainly, there is much more wrestling to do. These examples can at least support Woolf's contention that the mind is androgynous; and that one may write with the male or female side uppermost, no matter what one's biological sex may be.

The fact that Tiptree's style can be labelled 'masculine' in the first place must bring us back, though, to the realization that there *is* such a thing as a masculine style. It is not confined to men; it certainly is not one that is written by all men. It is not a style 'natural' to men, but one that is artificially created. Moreover, its nature as a masculine style is not absolute but relative. Because of the elusiveness of both style and sex, it will never be possible to pinpoint objectively the 'masculinity' of a piece of writing. One attempt at objectivity in this area of sexual styles is Mary Hiatt's book on *The Way Women Write* (New York: Teachers College Press, 1977). She uses a computer to test the validity of stereotypes about women's writing. Her samples are taken from fifty works by men and fifty by women, equally divided between fiction and non-fiction. Some of the assumed characteristics of women's writing she investigates in these samples are: long-windedness, as measured by sentence length; lack of balance, as indicated by the number of parallel constructions; emotionality, as indicated by the presence of certain key adverbs; and 'shrillness', reflected in use of the exclamation point. Hiatt finds that the stereotypes simply do not apply; and in general 'the style of the women writers appears conservative, somewhat cautious, and moderate as compared with the style of the men writers.' (p. 124). Whether this is a woman's 'natural' style is another question: Hiatt suggests that the chief reason for this sort of moderation is 'that women are a minority group, more likely to conform than to dare'. (p. 136). Quite aside from any doubts about method, the computer leaves us finally with the old problem of interpretation. It provides us with no settled conclusions about the 'natural' writing style of men and women. Such conclusions are probably impossible, certainly undesirable; and this book will not supply them. Instead it will deal with several different attempts to create the artifice that is a masculine style.

All of these attempts have been made in the twentieth century, under the pressure of the new self-consciousness noted by Woolf. The authors considered are a deliberately limited group, a group of extreme cases selected as for a laboratory experiment. Because they are extreme, characteristics which are normally diffuse and elusive may show up more clearly. I have looked for male authors dealing explicitly with the masculine role, or at least with masculine activity. The subject matter of their work is thus self-conscious to begin with. But in nearly every case self-consciousness extends further to the realm of style. For these authors, it is premature to say that the style is the man. The man is in the process of being made, and a style is one way of making his manhood. As style becomes a conscious sexual strategy, it tells us more about masculinity than does subject matter. Studying subject matter alone, books may too easily be viewed as casebooks, a happy hunting ground for Men We Disapprove Of and Good Guys. Literary criticism degenerates into gossip. By emphasizing style instead we may gain insight into what Woolf calls 'the weight, the pace, the stride of a man's mind' – the subtlest rhythms and convolutions of masculine experience.

Those authors who are consciously exploring the idea of a masculine style were once referred to by Shulamith Firestone as a 'new Virility School' in twentieth-century literature.[28] The phrase is a useful shorthand, though it should not raise any expectations that I will trace a school in the usual historical sense. This could be done, of course. In America the School of Virility is sired by Papa Hemingway and is now in its third generation. It includes such writers as Norman Mailer, Philip Roth, James Dickey, Frederick Exley and – the new generation – Jim Harrison and Tom McGuane. The phenomenon I am dealing with, however, is internationally diffused; and this is reflected in the varied selection here. If an author is not obsessed with masculinity throughout his career, like Yukio Mishima, he at least devotes one work to this obsession, as do Alfred Jarry, Alberto Moravia and Michel Leiris. Taking manhood as their subject matter, these men work out on paper their responses to the adjustment called for by their historical situation.

At the same time that they are writing about manhood, these authors are living it. Most of them follow the role as their culture has shaped it, in its commonest form. No experience, of course, is so common that it should be taken for granted; it is part of the artist's responsibility to make us fully perceive the nature of things we have never questioned. Still, it is curious that men of intelligence and sensitivity should aspire to a role which is a kind of lowest common denominator – a role in which sensitivity is suspect and intelligence (except for a certain practical kind) simply irrelevant. Montaigne, in the *Apologie de Raimond Sebond*, admits that his intelligence is no match for the natural virility of a muleteer. Similarly, writers like Norman Mailer, Ernest Hemingway and Frederick Exley are in competition with any street-corner tough, because they have willingly placed themselves in his territory, on his terms. This extends even to the territory where writers should have the most expertise, that of language; for the masculine role designates a certain toughness of language as appropriate.

Accordingly, this book begins by examining the ways in which the language of men serves as a model for Mailer's shifting styles. The chapters that follow often centre around one author, but are essentially about various aspects of masculine style, in particular as these relate to content. So the idea of manly reserve is given in two versions and balanced with its opposite, the hyperbolical; the tough is balanced with the dandified. Such enormous variations in style are nevertheless unified in unexpected ways, and arise as alternative solutions to the same problematical situation. The relation of literary style to life style is explored throughout – through considerations of body image, through analysis of masculine role-playing, and finally through the problem of male autobiography. Though the chapters are linked, they remain various in the end; and this is as it should be. No variety will be enough to exhaust the subject, for each man negotiates his own version of manhood.

It is a fair generalization, however, to say that in each of these men self-consciousness undermines their masculine assertion. Beneath the blatant *machismo* one finds considerable ambivalence towards the traditional masculine role. These writers recognize not only the role's power and its sense of archetypal fulfilment, but also its limitations, its self-deceptions, its destructiveness. What is said about life style applies just as much to the literary style of these authors. No matter what masculine style they develop, it tends to question itself, even destroy itself. A writer's concentration on the sexual is not always 'fatal', as Woolf would have it. However, it does impede a full vision of experience: Yukio Mishima, in deciding to pursue a purely masculine style, comments that 'any truths that might be overlooked as a result were no concern of mine.'[29] These virile writers have a vision that is necessarily partial; and because it is partial, some may even consider it false. Nevertheless to examine that vision can teach us something of value, something about men and women alike. We are all of us creatures of partial vision.

CHAPTER 1

The language of men

'A good novelist,' Norman Mailer has said, 'can do without everything but the remnant of his balls.'[1] This is the kind of statement we have grown accustomed to hearing from Mailer – so accustomed, in fact, that we may dismiss it as merely another outrageous way of advertising himself. If we take the statement seriously we will indignantly sputter out names like Austen, Bronte, Woolf. . . . This reaction is no more to the point: the good novelist Mailer really has in mind is Mailer. And in any attempt to understand Mailer's work, this statement has to be taken into account. It points to an intimate relation between the *macho* postures of his life and the nature of his literary art. In 1971 Norman Mailer, of all people, agreed to join a men's consciousness-raising group. After some second thoughts he sent this note to the man who had invited him:

> . . . Frankly a men's consciousness-raising session does not interest me much. I'm leery of that and sex discussions and all such apparatus, if you will, for I think it's a way of digging too close to the source of one's work. Obviously I would rather write a good book than go around raising my consciousness. If you think the two go together, I'm not at all certain I agree. Man is verily a bag and when he blows out in one place, caves in at the other.[2]

Manhood is 'close to the source' of Mailer's work – so close that its nature must be allowed to elude him if it is to continue its creative influence. Of course Mailer is constantly talking about the nature of manhood. Yet the way that he talks about it always falls short of a coherent, comprehensive definition. This is partly a matter of choice, for the reasons given in his note. Partly, too, it is a matter of necessity when dealing with something that Mailer considers not a state but a process.

'Masculinity is not something given to you, something you're born with, but something you gain,' says Mailer in *Cannibals and Christians*. 'And you gain it by winning small battles with honor.'[3] The statement looks backward to *Advertisements for Myself*, where Mailer writes that 'being a man is the continuing battle of one's life.'[4] It looks forward to *The Armies of the Night* in which 'Nobody was born a man; you earned manhood provided you were good enough, bold enough.'[5] And beyond this there is the comment in *The Prisoner of Sex* that 'a man can hardly ever assume he has become a man – in the instant of such complacency he may be on the way to becoming less masculine.'[6] Spanning a good part of Mailer's career thus far, these statements add up to a kind of Kierkegaardian fear and trembling – only what is feared is fear itself, or any equivalent betrayal of one's masculinity. The god here is manhood; and like any god, it eludes definition.

Only once has he tackled head-on the question of 'what is a man? and what indeed is the passion to be masculine?' The answers Mailer gives in *The Prisoner of Sex* only raise more questions. He finds it 'reasonable to assume that the primary quality of man was an assertion, and on the consequence an isolation, that one had to alienate oneself from nature to become a man, step out of nature, be almost as if opposed to nature, be perhaps directly opposed to nature. . . .' The conclusion to be drawn from this brings him round to familiar territory again: it is that 'man was a spirit of unrest who proceeded to become less masculine whenever he ceased to strive'.[7] But let us return to the first sentence and see what happens to Mailer's style when he is on less familiar territory. The sentence has a curious construction which might be illuminated by considering it as sexual: Mailer finds it necessary to nudge and inch his way towards full penetration of the mystery. The comparison becomes less gratuitous when we recall Mailer's idea that women, because 'natural', are closer to the mystery. They are then appropriate emblems of all mystery confronted by the embattled male – including, para-doxically, the mystery of his own manhood, in so far as it is mysterious. In Mailer's view, as in Goethe's, the eternal feminine draws us on – only with Mailer the eternal feminine, or Great Bitch, is something to be subdued and conquered. The means of conquering is 'that equivalent of a phallus, that ghost phallus of the mentality, firm strong-tongued ego'.[8]

These attitudes carry over to Mailer's art in a peculiar way. The Great Bitch is also the novel, according to Mailer; and the proudest boast of any writer who takes on that form is 'Man, I made her moan.'[9] The muse must be subdued and mastered by the male, like any other woman. If not, she is likely to cost him the mastery of his own manhood. Richard Poirier has suggested that Mailer's choice of topics, 'being as they are invariably and conspicuously masculine, is a sort of anticipatory compensation for the feminine exercise of delivering these topics to the world.'[10]

But what, one might ask, is 'feminine' about the exercise of writing? Nearly everything, according to certain common views. A real man is supposed to be a doer, a man of action. 'Deeds are masculine, words are feminine,' runs an Italian proverb. Another proverb, Scottish this time, claims that 'Nothing is so unnatural as a talkative man or a quiet woman.' So a man who speaks much is suspect; and he is hardly less suspect if he happens to speak well. One linguistic study to determine what kind of words were considered 'effeminate' found that students, especially males, 'equated culture and effeminacy'.[11] In the traditional stereotype, of course, the woman is the guardian of culture. A man must not, then, cast doubt on his virility by being too articulate, betraying too great a consciousness of language. It is considered finicky and feminine to be concerned about the details of speech. 'When you see a fellow careful about his words, and neat in his speech,' warns Seneca, 'know this for a certainty: that man's mind is busied about toys, there's no solidity in him.' (Moral Epistle 115) In short, he is not a doer. If he were, he would not have any undue respect for language.

I realize that this notion of language as effeminate runs directly counter to much feminist criticism. Gilbert and Gubar's *The Madwoman in the Attic*, for instance, describes an 'anxiety of authorship' felt by nineteenth-century women writers when intruding upon a male domain. Far from being natural talkers, these women were, in Marge Piercy's words, 'unlearning to not speak'. We must keep in mind, though, that this book deals with 'the first era in which female authorship was no longer in some sense anomalous'. In the twentieth century 'women do now attempt the pen with energy and authority.'[12] And their energy is often pitted against what they see as the masculine bias of language – not only its built-in sexism, but the supposed gender of language itself. Hélène Cixous feels that 'language conceals an invincible adversary because it's the language of men and their grammar.'[13] Her reference to 'speech which has been governed by the phallus' aligns her with those feminists who have reacted angrily to Jacques Lacan's neo-Freudian idea of 'the phallus as signifier'. It is not enough to warn against confusing this purely symbolical phallus with the real penis. A philosophical system is always constructed on a metaphor.[14] Metaphors such as this one, and that of language as the 'Absence-of-the-Father', while not invalidating Lacan's theories, may evoke a justifiable wariness in feminists.

My own wariness is more general: I distrust all attempts to assign a gender to language. Inevitably these tell us less about language than about the state of mind of those who are assigning a gender to it. If we clearly understand that we are studying the perceivers rather than the language they perceive, then there is value in examining these attempts. My purpose here will not be to decide whether language is 'really' masculine or feminine. It may be either or both, depending on who is doing the perceiving. Let us try to imagine, then, the perceptions of Mailer and his ilk.

I have indicated how in this century a new self-consciousness may have given rise to a male 'anxiety of authorship'. It matters little whether that anxiety is widely spread or not; I am only concerned with its effect on a small group which is trying to straddle both the macho and the literary. For such men, Lacan's theories will be of small comfort. We are not dealing with the heady reaches of higher criticism, but with folk knowledge: what every man knows and no man can afford not to know. Words admittedly can be used as a form of male display, as patriarchal–verbal imperialism. Still, this does not counterbalance the stubborn street knowledge that a man who uses big words isn't likely to be very tough.

> the boys i mean are not refined
> they cannot chat of that and this
> they do not give a fart for art
> they kill like you would take a piss

So. e.e. cummings describes the nature of tough-guys' turf.

For Mailer, it is extremely important to be tough. A special urgency consequently informs his need to master the muse. His devotion to manhood runs a certain risk of contamination through the act of writing, even when Mailer is writing about manhood. Like any consciously 'manly' writer, his situation is paradoxical: he asserts his manhood in a way that the 'real' man considers unmanly. If such a writer wishes to resolve the paradox on a masculine note, selection of subject matter is effective only to a degree. More effective is the writer's choice of style, for here he may grapple with words themselves in an attempt to alter their 'feminine' nature.

Above all Mailer is a stylist – according to some, the foremost of his time. The source of his style is his own deepest self: Mailer speaks of 'the yaws of conscience a writer learns to feel when he sets his mirrors face to face and begins to jiggle his Self for a style which will have some relation to *him*.'[15] That deepest self is so involved with the idea of manhood that it would be surprising if there were no relation between Mailer's style of manhood and his literary style. The fact is that Mailer's style often draws on a subset of language opposed to the notion that words in general are effeminate. This subset is a distinct language of men.

There are, of course, popular stereotypes of the language of men as opposed to that of women. Like most stereotypes, these have limited validity: current research indicates that the stereotypes assume more differentiation than is actually the case.[16] Still, actual differences do exist, which linguists are only beginning to study systematically. For instance, certain adjectives are sex-linked: a man who uses words like *lovely* or *sweet* runs the risk of lowering his masculinity quotient. Otto Jesperson may have been the first to raise the problem of sex-related language differences in a chapter on 'The Woman' which he included in his *Language* (1921). The chapter is notorious for its patronizing attitude towards women, but is rich in hypotheses which are still being investigated. One of the most interesting of these deals with sentence construction by males and females. According to Jesperson, men use more complicated constructions, building sentences 'like a set of Chinese boxes', with clauses nesting one within another in patterns of subordination. Coordination is the distinctive feature of women's speech; their sentences are like 'a set of pearls joined together on a string of *ands* and similar words'.[17] Recent studies seem to bear out the more frequent use of the conjunction by women, but reveal as well that women are far more likely than men to be interrupted when conversing with the opposite sex.[18] Men may launch into complicated constructions just because they may be reasonably sure of finishing them; whereas women's constructions must allow them to stop at almost any point. If we turn to literature we seem to have a good example of the influence of women's speech on women's writing in the *ands* which stitch together Virginia Woolf's sentence:

> . . . she had known happiness, exquisite happiness, intense happiness, and it silvered the rough waves a little more brightly, as daylight faded, and the blue went out of the sea and it rolled in waves of pure lemon which curved and swelled and broke upon the beach and the ecstasy burst in her eyes and waves of pure delight raced over the floor of her mind and she felt, It is enough! It is enough!

The cadence is reminiscent of the close of Molly Bloom's soliloquy. It is accounted for in both cases not by considerations of sex but of content. Both passages describe a sudden rush and release of emotion in a kind of epiphany. Mailer uses a similar construction to render Larry Schiller's epiphany in *The Executioner's Song*;[19] and the effect is the more startling for the deliberate restraint of the writing in the rest of the novel. Another 'male' example of sentences strung together with *and* is the opening of *A Farewell to Arms*. There the *and* was said by Hemingway to function like the base note in a Bach prelude,[20] and is far from having any overtones of effeminacy. In literature as well as in actual speech, then, there are still problems in supporting hypotheses like Jesperson's.

Other hypotheses, with no more initial support, can be backed up by systematic research. An example is George Steiner's comment on women's speech:

> At a rough guess, women's speech is richer than men's in those shadings of desire and futurity known in Greek and Sanskrit as optative; women seem to verbalize a wider range of qualified resolve and masked promise. Feminine uses of the subjunctive in European languages give to material facts and

relations a characteristic *vibrato*. I do not say that they lie about
the obtuse, resistant fabric of the world: they multiply the
facets of reality, they strengthen the adjective to allow it an
alternative nominal status, in a way which men often find
unnerving.[21]

Steiner's 'rough guess' is corroborated by linguists who find that
women's speech has an aversion to strong statements. Consequently the habitual use of various 'hedges' ('sort of', 'I guess'); of
the 'tag-question' ('the service here is awful, isn't it?'); of the
rising intonation which usually signifies a question, used by
women when giving answers. Generally women speak with a
wider range of intonation patterns of all kinds than men do. They
communicate more by pitch and stress; as Robin Lakoff puts it,
'women speak in italics' more than men.[22] This is not to say that
men's speech is the norm, that it is neutral – though at times an
ostentatious neutrality can be made into one of the strongest
characteristics of male speech.

In fact, the norm is women's speech, according to Robin
Lakoff:

> Since the mother and other women are the dominant
> influences in the lives of most children under the age of five,
> probably both boys and girls first learn 'women's language' as
> their first language. . . . As they grow older, boys especially
> go through a stage of rough talk, as described by Spock and
> others. . . . By the time children are ten or so, and split up
> into same-sex peer groups, the two languages are already
> present. . . . But it seems that what has happened is that the
> boys have unlearned their original form of expression, and
> adopted new forms of expression, while the girls retain their
> old ways of speech.[23]

The new forms of expression which the young males have
adopted may be summed up in the phrase 'rough talk', an
umbrella phrase which covers a number of male characteristics of
speech.

Obscene speech, first, will be most alarming to many parents.
While the use of obscenity by young girls is viewed with strong
disapproval, an attitude of 'boys will be boys' (whatever that
means) may excuse the male child who adopts obscene expres-

sions. In some cases, a boy may be viewed as 'cute' in his babyish attempts to wield the talismans of male power. For obscene words *are* talismans. Such is the attitude of Henry Miller, who uses these words not just as 'technical devices' but as 'magical terms'. To him, 'the uses of obscenity offer an equivalent to the uses of the miraculous in the Masters.'[24] At this time, the chances are still slim that a woman would be making such an assertion – an assertion which, from a man, seems more convincing because we detect in it a familiar boyish glee.

A related roughness in language is found in the greater use of slang among males. The editor of the *Dictionary of American Slang* claims that 'most American slang is created and used by males.' Because slang words refer primarily to male interests, he says, 'the majority of entries in this dictionary could be labelled "primary masculine use".'[25] For Jesperson, slang is a secondary sexual characteristic. Exactly the same opinion is held by Jean Genet. For the patterns of domination between 'males' and 'females' in his homosexual world accurately mirror, as Kate Millett has shown, the patterns in the world outside his own. This extends even to the patterns of language.

> Slang was for men. It was the male tongue. Like the language
> of men among the caribees, it became a secondary sexual
> attribute. It was like the colored plumage of male birds, like
> the multi-colored silk garments which are the prerogatives of
> the warriors of the tribe. It was a crest and spurs. Everyone
> could understand it, but the only ones who could speak it
> were the men who at birth received as a gift the gestures, the
> carriage of the hips, legs and arms, the eyes, the chest, with
> which one can speak it.[26]

If men naturally gravitate to slang, women gravitate merely to euphemism, if we are to believe Jesperson, because of their 'instinctive shrinking from coarse and gross expressions'.[27] Needless to say, any woman could disprove this statement in an instant, and it might move many to do so. It is, however, true that women use slang less often than men: recent research has shown that women do put more emphasis on correct speech. The reasons why this should be so are less clear. Henley and Thorne remind us that 'greater circumspection in behavior often accompanies subordination.'[28] Lacking genuine status, women may be inclined to put more value on the symbols of status, such as correct speech. One linguist has suggested that 'while men can be rated socially on what they *do*, women may be rated primarily on how they *appear* – so their speech is important.'[29] The conservatism that Hiatt found in women's writing may be accounted for in the same way.

A man, on the other hand, may revel in bad grammar: as long as it is thrown off with enough verbal swagger, it is merely another of the 'working-class forms' which so widely symbolize virility. Even little boys know this, which helps to explain why their pronunciation is so much more careless and slurred than that of little girls. They drop their g's, for instance; they say *goin'* and *runnin'* like little Bob Dylans. They also make more grammatical errors than do girls. And with this kind of 'rough talk' boys of all ages assert that they are men. Less intimidated by correctness of speech, men are as a result more free to experiment. Jesperson considers them 'the chief renovators of language' not only in slang but in literary forms as well. A writer like Aeschylus is then appropriately praised for 'the fearless masculine licence with which he handled the most flexible of languages'.[30] Licence in language is itself a masculine prerogative.

There is then a distinct language of men. As I have already admitted, it may be less distinct from women's speech than is generally assumed. The distinctions may be exaggerated to suit a prevailing stereotype. Still, if a stereotype exists, it may be used: the language of men, at the very least, may be adopted for special occasions. And it is so adopted by men who otherwise speak a very different language, when they are thrown together in such masculine arenas as the locker room, the army training camp, the stag party, the hunting trip, the pub crawl – any occasion when men are conscious of the need to assert their masculine bond. If it is used like this by ordinary men, it may be used as well by writers who have been made conscious of their need for it.

Mailer has been more conscious than most of the existence of a language of men; he has even used that phrase as the title of a short story. In 'The Language of Men' an army cook is systematically excluded from the fellowship of the men in his company and made the butt of their jokes. His resentment erupts when he is asked to donate a can of oil for a fish fry to which he has not been invited. He refuses. When the angry men confront him, things escalate to the point when the cook realizes he must fight one of them, a big Southerner. His heart in his mouth, he lunges forward – and the fight is stopped. This is a turning point in his relationship with the men. He even becomes friends with the Southerner. Eventually he admits to his friend that he hadn't really wanted to fight him on that day; and with that admission he realizes he has lost his new friendship. Not all has been lost, of course: 'He was no longer so worried about becoming a man; he felt that to an extent he had become one. But in his heart he wondered if he would ever learn the language of men.' It is significant that Mailer, himself a former army cook, can make such a distinction between manhood and its language. It indicates his awareness that many of the codes of masculinity to which he subscribes are artificial.

The language of men, in the short story by that name, has more to do with psychological gesture and stance than with the use of words. When we turn to Mailer's use of words, though, we find that many of the stances of his style, and his switches of style, become more comprehensible as versions of the spoken language of men. The common characteristics of that language influence Mailer's use of words in modest ways at first; and then they flower in his hands into something rich and strange.

The first example of such influence will hardly seem so dramatic to us as it did to Mailer. It is the rewriting of *The Deer Park* in such a way as to roughen the cultivated style of a narrator who originally sounded rather like Nick Carraway. Switching from Fitzgerald to Hemingway, Mailer made throughout the entire manuscript a series of small alterations. In the original a sentence reads 'I wished to set Eitel at the place nearest my feet, vizier to the potentate, and it charmed me that in my first big affair I should be so proficient.' In the new version this becomes '. . . I wanted to set Eitel at my feet, second to the champion. It pleased me in my big affair that I had such a feel for the ring.' 'We soon developed another dispute' becomes 'we soon found something new to fight about.' To the original sentences Mailer often added terse clipped afterthoughts: 'There I went from the Air Force to look for a good time. Some time ago.' Or, later: 'And she gave me a sisterly kiss. Older sister.' Mailer describes the process like this:

. . . the style of the work lost its polish, became rough, and I can say real, because there was an abrupt and muscular body back of the voice now. It had been there all the time, trapped in the porcelain of a false style, but now as I chipped away . . . I felt as if finally I was learning how to write, learning the joints of language and the touch of a word, felt as if I came close to the meanings of sound and could say which of two close words was more female or more forward.[31]

Whenever Mailer has the choice between two close words he chooses the 'more forward' rather than the 'more female' of the two. The distinction between them is made in accordance with the common feeling that cultivated words are unmanly. Again, the introduction of short sentence fragments flouts the grammatical precision which, in a certain male view, is the province of the fussy and effeminate. These bitten-off words evoke the tough-guy, side-of-the-mouth delivery characteristic of movie detectives and gangsters. In Mailer's own movies, he has played both types with an evident relish in their language – made so much his own by now that he can improvise in it with facility. It is no longer merely a matter of roughened speech, but of the flagrantly male use of slang and obscenity.

Mailer swings out daringly into this area of speech in a *Partisan Review* article on Vietnam which winds up with 'Mr. J., Mr. L.B.J., Boss Man of Show Biz – I salute you in your White House Oval; I mean America will shoot all over the shithouse wall if this jazz goes on, Jim.'[32] The sentence has a freakish, creative use of obscenity; hip rhythms; a complex self-mockery, like that of urban blacks, enveloping a serious, even menacing communication. It anticipates the style as well as the theme of Mailer's next novel, *Why Are We in Vietnam?* The book takes the venerable theme of the Hunt as initiation to manhood and twists it to bring out the potent, ambivalent competitiveness between the men involved. The hero, eighteen-year-old D.J., is a self-proclaimed genius who forms part of his father's *entourage* on a big hunt in the wilds of Alaska. D.J.'s father is a corporation executive who exemplifies the worst of that breed and some of the best. Predictably he feels that his masculinity is on the line if he fails to bring back the head of a grizzly bear. During the hunt, D.J. enacts with his father the bitter oedipal rivalry which is a recurrent theme in

Mailer's novels. D.J. also passes through the temptation to steal the manhood of his friend Tex by sodomizing him. Instead the two become blood brothers – brothers in blood in a special sense. For as the novel closes, both are on their way to Vietnam, fulfilling the 'will to kill' that they have sensed in the psychic and electrical currents of the frozen North. Those flickering currents are evoked throughout by the radio-land slang of D.J., Disc Jockey of the mind and narrator of the whole novel. Here is the opening paragraph:

> Hip hole and hupmobile, Braunschweiger, you didn't invite Geiger and his counter for nothing, here is D.J. the friendLee voice at your service – hold tight young America – introductions come. Let go of my dong, Shakespeare, I have gone too long, it is too late to tell my tale, may Batman tell it, let him declare there's blood on my dick and D.J. Dicktor Doc Dick and Jek has got the bloods, and has done animal murder, out out damn fart, and murder of the soldierest sort, cold was my hand and hot.

The slang is effective in a number of ways simultaneously. It is the creative language of the hipster, swinging freely from one association to another. It is the anarchic language of the outsider – D.J. teases us with the possibility that he is really a spade putting us on from Harlem. But not least, slang is the flaunting of a male prerogative in a novel explicitly preoccupied with the definition and attainment of manhood.

The obscenity follows naturally along the same lines, and is a vigorous, virile force throughout the book. John Aldridge has suggested that the purpose of the obscenity is 'to help alleviate the psychological pressures that have driven us to commit the atrocity of Vietnam.'[33] Certainly there is some such cathartic element present. But obscenity is also the mainspring of a peculiarly masculine creativity exemplified by both D.J. and Mailer. 'Obscenity', Mailer declares, 'has nothing to do any longer with revelations of the sexual act . . . no, obscenity is rather become a style of speech, a code of manners, a transmission belt for humor and violence.' Speaking of the improvised dialogue of a film he made, Mailer defends its use of four-letter words: 'The obscenity loosened stores of improvisation, gave a beat to the sound, opened the actors to figures of speech – creativity is always next to the *verboten*.'[34]

The last comment is thrown off, but should not so quickly be thrown aside. It implies a psychological need to flout the rules, to push past limits for no reason other than that they *are* limits. The writer courts the sensation of danger and sees it as a fructifying influence in his art. Rather like a sudden surge of adrenalin, that sensation may alert and focus his senses, may allow him to accomplish feats that would be impossible to him in ordinary circumstances. An example is the sentence Mailer uses to conclude the article on Vietnam. When he reprints the article in *Cannibals and Christians* he observes – with, one suspects, a touch of pride – 'Its last sentence is not uncertain to damage a general welcome for this book.' Yet it is just this sentence, with its sensation of danger, which becomes the creative seed of his next novel. The thirst for danger is characteristic of a common type of male who must always be testing himself. Mailer's affinities to the type are indicated by his notion that

> even if one dulled one's talent in the punishment of becoming a man, it was more important to be a man than a very good writer, that probably I could not become a very good writer unless I learned first how to keep my nerve, and what is more difficult, learned how to find more of it.[35]

Writing is an arena in which one fights the continuing battle of manhood. One fights in order to acquire more nerve, and acquires it for no other purpose but to have that nerve, which is so large a part of being a man. More nerve does not appear unless circumstances demand it. Consequently a writer like Mailer will repeatedly place himself in dangerous circumstances, no matter what the particular version of danger may be.

Obscenity we have seen to be one such particular version. Another version is the surrealism in Mailer's writing. 'Surrealism' is a fair enough label to give this tendency in Mailer: it is the label he himself affixes to Henry Miller in reference to the same tendency: '. . . surrealistic Henry, Prince-poet of Dada, knave-acrobat of the cosmos. Now he will string a zither across Tania's immortal navel once more and shit his metaphysical arpeggios.'[36] The last sentence may serve as our first example. Mailer, himself a 'knave-acrobat', has surely taken a tumble here. The elements of shit, metaphysics and arpeggios remain disparate, desperately clutching at originality. Yet the sentence does not just quietly expire: it twitches with a grotesque nervous life, like a galvanized frog. If we are aware of the sentence's failure, we are also aware of its daring. Indeed, it is only if the threat of failure – that is, of danger – occasionally realizes itself that we are given the sense of daring. That sense need not always be a part of surrealism. Often, as in the best of Henry Miller, surrealistic writing has a crystalline, almost classic quality; the words seem inevitable. In Mailer, though, the surrealistic phrases call attention to themselves. They strut their stuff with schoolboy bravado. Often, as in the above example, they come down to that cheap surrealism which is merely mixed metaphor. Memory is 'never a wall but more a roulette of the most extraordinary events and the most insignificant, all laced into the same vessel.'[37] A sexual climax is 'hot as the gates of an icy slalom.'[38] Such failures are the price it is necessary to pay for the successes, when part of the exhilaration of success is the consciousness of danger overcome. Here is a success: Mailer reports on Barry Goldwater interrupting himself during a speech:

> 'Hi, honey,' he sang out like a traveling salesman, which brought a titter from the delegation, for his voice had shifted too quickly, the codpiece was coming off, Rain and the Reverend Davidson. Something skinny, itchy, hard as a horselaugh, showed – he was a cannoneer with a hairy ear. Goldwater went on, the good mood continued. . . .[39]

An apparently unplanned spattering of images is in fact locked tightly together. What is 'skinny, itchy, hard' is not just a streak in Goldwater's personality, but also that which is behind the codpiece. Then 'hard as a horselaugh' pivots the emphasis back to the vulgar, folksy style of the travelling salesman – and back again, to the codpiece, since he is the hero of innumerable dirty jokes. The 'cannoneer with a hairy ear' offers more sexual imagery behind a final folksy stance. Sound and rhythm smooth it all together. And finally this short surrealistic freak of style accurately reflects a real flash of embarrassment and the sense of danger.

A simple academic close reading thus allows this selection to pass with high marks. Why, we ask ourselves, can't Mailer apply such a test to all his work? The answer is that he probably doesn't want to. For Mailer, who aspires to be Renaissance man

in so many other respects, is a practitioner of Renaissance *sprezzatura*. Castiglione asserts that *sprezzatura*, or nonchalance, is the
pre-eminent virtue in all one's actions. To be seen to labour in
anything deprives a man of credit; whereas admiration doubles if
he seems to throw it off without effort or forethought. Mailer
quite regularly flaunts the offhand nature of his work: for
instance, he boasts that what he is publishing is a first draft,
written at the tail end of a drunken binge.[40] He lets us know that
Why Are We in Vietnam? was written in only four months. He
announces in *Esquire* that he is going to write *An American Dream*
in serial instalments, each instalment to be finished just before
deadline. Moreover, he has his hero kill his wife in the very first
instalment. This, he tells the press, 'is like taking off your clothes
in Macy's window. What do you do next? But finally I realized I
was the one man in America who could do it. The clue to me is, I
figure I've got as much physical courage as the next guy, but I'm
profoundly afraid of being a moral coward.'[41] The composition
of *An American Dream* is then more than 'existential'; it is downright dangerous. By throwing off his work with so little revision,
Mailer is as it were performing his acrobatics without a safety net.
The performance as a result becomes more breath-taking for the
reader. For the writer, the risk calls forth more reserves of nerve
and leaves him more of a man.

Words, which are commonly opposed to acts, are in this way
made by Mailer into a species of manly action. The interplay
between words and actions has been continuous throughout his
career. His own actions figure prominently in many of his 'true-
life novels' – though sometimes, as in *The Prisoner of Sex*, the
actions come down to the sheer act of writing the book we are
reading. His words speak of his actions; his actions realize his
words. In 1957 Mailer writes an essay entitled 'The White Negro'
in which he asserts that one must free the psychopath in oneself,
committing murder if necessary in order to guarantee existential
freedom. In 1960 he stabs his second wife without, however,
killing her. In 1964 he begins *An American Dream* with Rojack's
murder of his wife as the necessary price of his spiritual survival.
The intimate relation between these episodes, Judith Fetterley
says, makes reading Mailer an experience like no other: '. . . as
art merges into action, so action merges into art, and the result is
An American Dream, whose metaphoric frenzy seems like the

afterbirth of an aborted action, as if metaphor expands in precisely the same degree to which action has been limited.'[42] The
expanded metaphor, as we have noted earlier, may be seen itself
as a kind of action, and a dangerous action at that. It is essential
that Mailer see his writing in such ways if he is to suffer no losses
in the continuing battle for manhood.

Mailer's style is thus in many respects an extraordinary version of the ordinary language of men, having its rough edges, its
slang and obscenity, its stance of devil-may-care recklessness,
and always a felt undercurrent of action. This is not to say that
Mailer's style reduces to this set of common characteristics.
Rather the common characteristics are illuminated by Mailer's
subtle use of them. His use of the language of men is distin-
guished from the norm by more than just superior imagination
and verbal facility. Male slang and obscenity, after all, may often
be quite creative, a model for Mailer in his cinematic impro-
visions. No, what most distinguishes Mailer's language from that
of mainstream *machismo* is his consciousness of the language of
men *as* a language. It is a consciousness that one usually has for a
foreign language, one which men like Mailer's army cook must
work at learning to speak well. Mailer, though he speaks the
language very well indeed, is always slightly alienated by virtue
of his consciousness of it.

Any consciousness of manhood (besides mere self-congratulation) implies a female element, a place just outside of manhood
from which to view its contours. And so no one fights the battle
for manhood more passionately than one who is highly conscious of manhood's nature. He senses that very consciousness
in him as a female element, and 'the feminine in his nature cries
out for proof he is a man'.[43] We hardly associate the feminine
with Mailer's nature, but that does not mean it isn't there. He was
bewildered by the fact that his first person narrators up till *The
Deer Park* were 'over-delicate, oversensitive, and painfully
tender, which was an odd portrait to give, because I was not
tender, not physically; when it was a matter of strength I had as
much as the next man.'[44] The tender, 'overdelicate' narrators of
his first novels may reflect an aspect of their author in spite of his
objections that he was not tender – 'not physically'. When Mailer
asserts, then, that 'a firm erection on a delicate fellow was the
adventurous juncture of ego and courage',[45] he himself may be

the delicate fellow in question. Certainly ego and courage are largely responsible for the potency of his writing, for the fact that words become for him a 'ghost phallus' rather than the stigma of effeminacy. Mailer's relationship to maleness is consequently not a straightforward thing; it is supple, paradoxical, the joy and despair of his critics. 'Mailer, of course, makes a fetish of being male,' Fetterley observes; 'but what gives his fetishism its unique quality is the fact that it is impossible to determine to what degree it is parody and to what degree it is endorsement. Mailer is the embodiment of what he criticizes and the criticism of what he embodies.'[46]

Sometimes the contradictions in Mailer's position emerge with unusual clarity. An instance is his comment on the nature of books written for men. 'The world of a man is a world of surface slick and rock knowledge,' he says.

> A man must live by daily acts where he goes to work and works on the world some incremental bit, using the tools, instruments, and the techniques of the world. Thus a man cannot afford to go too deeply into the underlying meaning of a single subject. He prefers to become interested in quick proportions and contradictions, in the practical surface of things.[47]

It is interesting to compare his version of masculine perception with Josephine Donovan's idea of feminine perception: her hypothesis that women see as important that which lies *beneath* the surface of things. The feminine perception is inward-oriented, whereas here Mailer's idea of masculine perception is that it is outward-oriented.[48] Mailer finds that *Catch-22*, *Naked Lunch* and *The Thin Red Line* all share, beneath their dissimilarities, this quality of writing directed at men. But a few pages earlier he has criticized *The Thin Red Line* for precisely that attention to surface and technicality which he is now denominating male. Jones's book gave him only a kind of satisfaction,

> as if one had studied geology for a semester and now knew more. I suppose what was felt lacking was the curious sensuousness of combat, the soft lift of awe and pleasure that one was moving out onto the rim of the dead. If one was not too tired, there were times when a blade of grass coming out of

the ground before one's nose was as significant as the finger of Jehovah in the Sistine Chapel.

Jones fell short, Mailer concludes, 'when he kept the mystical side of his talents on bread and water, and gave his usual thoroughgoing company man's exhibition of how much he knows technically about his product. I think that is the mistake.'[49] The mistake, though, is one that is characterized as peculiarly male; and implied in Mailer's criticism of Jones's limits is a criticism of the limits of masculinity. It would be natural for Mailer to compare *The Thin Red Line* with his own *The Naked and the Dead*. But he sidesteps the comparison: he does not see them as similar enough to compare. His own novel 'is concerned more with characters than with military action,' he observes.[50] He might have added that in its attention to mood and evanescent states of being, as well as the 'sensuousness of combat', it has more of that mystical element which James Jones lacks.

This mystical element comes increasingly to the fore as Mailer's career progresses, and is explicitly elaborated in metaphysical essays on mood, on food, on time and the afterlife, on all manner of psychic odysseys. It is unwarranted to call this mysticism a 'female' element, but it is certainly the antithesis of the stress on surface which Mailer claims is characteristic of writing for men. The paradox is that this interest in mysticism accelerates at the same rate as Mailer's interest in manhood, and the two are often strange bedfellows. An extreme is reached in *An American Dream*. The surface of the plot is a charade of masculinity: Rojack subdues women by his sexual genius or, in the case of his wife, murders the bitch; he faces off or fights with an increasingly powerful series of men; he tempts death a dozen times. Yet for this tough guy, the real experience appears not to take place on the surface, but rather in some mystical realm. Rojack sizes up an opponent not as a problem in street-fighting techniques but as a psychological entity communicated by his smell. Smell is the dominant sense in the book. Its ineffable nature allows Mailer to use it as a metaphor for the subtlest psychic communication. In describing a smell he spins out labyrinthine associations which slow the moment and remove it far from its existence as surface alone. If we think in terms of the notion that man's attention is principally directed outward and woman's inward, we have a striking contradiction: an aggressively virile narrator with a feminine sensibility.

Sooner or later, contradictions such as these emerge in any attempt by a man to perceive his own masculinity. And contradictions emerge just as much in any exploration of the language of men. A lush grandiloquence like that which Mailer occasionally writes can have an effect of masculinity quite as much as a reserved, pruned-back prose like Hemingway's. It is all in the subtleties of the circumstances. When we are made conscious of the element of risk, then such a prose as Mailer's becomes a masculine act of daring, in which what is being dared is 'feminine gushiness'. Even when the prose seems to slip over the line, we cannot be sure that the style is wholly genuine. Mailer's writing style has in it a sizable element of self-mockery. Fascinated by the aesthetics of the put-on, he is not above writing a style that is itself a put-on, a parody of his usual style. The line between the two is hard to draw; at times it might be hard for Mailer himself to draw it. For if this author is continually eluding us, he must also in a sense elude himself. The existential author is a creature of process, breaking through even his own definitions of himself, as an insect breaks through and sheds its husk. One of those definitions of himself is his style – the style is the man. So Mailer, who so consciously labours to create a style, will frequently switch to another. Something in him hopes to 'trap the Prince of Truth in the act of switching a style'.[51] That truth has to do, as much as anything else, with the nature of his own manhood.

The shifts in Mailer's style reflect a shifting line of battle; and the battle is a psychological one with words themselves. The Great Bitch is conquered anew in each new work, but the triumph is short-lived: the adversary soon presents herself again, armed with new wiles. Words wait to seduce the writer and rob him of his manhood in the very act which he hopes will assure him of it. The language of men may indeed be called upon, but provides no easy solution. We still find in its use paradoxes, convolutions and restless fluctuations, reflecting above all an intense self-consciousness. These characteristics of Mailer are perhaps only extreme versions of those of masculinity in general at this time. Some of the fascination of Mailer for us is that he enacts, among other things, a whole new mode of experiencing maleness. We read him to find, beyond Mailer's explicit idea on manhood, beyond and through the language of men, something that has never been said about the situation of all men today.

CHAPTER 2

Reserve and its reverse

Mailer's short story 'The Time of her Time', originally meant to be the core of an ambitious novel, describes a most improbable bullfighting school in the heart of New York City. The narrator, when he is not in bars picking up his daily lay, is teaching his students *faenas* and *veronicas* – all the repertoire of classical passes with the cape. Only what his students are facing is not a bull but a pair of bull's horns mounted on a wheeled contraption which is trundled across the room by another student. The ludicrous effect may be deliberate, one of many possible ironies in a work that is usually read as outrageously straightforward male chauvinism. The bullfighting reference may also be Mailer's tribute to Ernest Hemingway, author of *Death in the Afternoon* and lifelong *aficionado* of the bull ring. It is tempting to suggest that the relation of the mechanical bull to the real one says something about the relation of Mailer to Hemingway. However, though Mailer has learned much from Hemingway, he has not learned his lessons mechanically. For instance, the treatment of smell in *An American Dream* originates with the chapter on the smell of death in *For Whom the Bell Tolls*, but Mailer sees the full possibilities of using smell throughout the novel as a way to render psychic essences. Most of all what he has learned from Hemingway is the idea of advertising himself through his writing. In this respect, Mailer says, 'every American writer who takes himself to be both major and *macho* must sooner or later give a *faena* which borrows from the self-love of a Hemingway style.'[1]

Mailer thus places Hemingway as Papa to a whole school of literary *machos*. He was so placed relatively early in his career, most notoriously in an acerbic review by Max Eastman:

. . . some circumstances seem to have laid upon Hemingway a continual sense of the obligation to put forth evidence of red-blooded masculinity. It must be made obvious not only in the swing of the big shoulders and the clothes he puts on, but in the stride of his prose style and the emotions he permits to come to the surface there. This trait of his character has been strong enough to form the nucleus of a new flavor in English literature, and it has moreover begotten a veritable school of fiction-writers – a literary style, you might say, of wearing false hair on the chest.[2]

Hemingway's answer to this took the form of a memorable encounter with Eastman in the offices of Scribners. Hemingway first ripped open his shirt to reveal an abundantly hairy chest, then unbuttoned Eastman's shirt to reveal a hairless one, slapped Eastman across the face with his own review and finally wrestled him to the ground – unfortunately, in the confusion, managing to land beneath his opponent.

Eastman's comment is typical of the way that most critics have perceived the relation between Hemingway's masculinity and his writing style: they notice that a connection exists, but do not opt to explore it. The reason for this may be that up till now we have had a blind spot where the masculine role is concerned, viewing it as something more simple than it really is. So there has been little incentive to pair it with that other simple thing, the style of Ernest Hemingway. Critics have concerned themselves with the complexities inherent in that simple style; but who has considered that the masculine role has its own kind of complexities, and that these could in any way correspond? Led to the brink of such a possibility, the critic shies away to abstractions of familiar and certified complexity, out of a fear that where masculinity is concerned, there is just not enough to say. An example is Mark Schorer:

The style which made Hemingway famous – with its ascetic suppression of ornament and figure, its insistence on the objective and unreflective (for good fighters do not talk), its habit of understatement (or sportsmen boast), the directness and brevity of its syntactical constructions, its muscularity . . . – this style is an exact transfiguration of Hemingway's moral attitude toward a peculiarly violent and chaotic experience.[3]

The list of characteristics is powerfully permeated with a male cast, which is even made explicit in the parenthetical comments. Yet when Schorer adds them up, the sum is not the masculine, but the moral. His concluding statement expresses the way that Hemingway's work is generally perceived; what is wrong with that perception is only that it is too general. There are 'subtler demarcations' to be found in Hemingway's masculine mode.

We may begin with quite unsubtle stories which survive from Hemingway's high school days. They deal with ostentatiously masculine themes: trappers in Northern Canada, boxing, and Michigan Indians. All have an element of violence in them, most extremely so in the story called 'Judgement of Manitou'. In this story, a trapper who suspects that his partner has stolen his wallet sets a trap for him. When he finds that the wallet was taken by a squirrel, he rushes down the trail, but it is too late. The wolves have been there before him: 'Two ravens left off picking at the shapeless something that had once been Dick Haywood, and flapped lazily into a neighboring spruce.' Some critics feel that Hemingway's 'unmistakable stamp' is already present in these early stories: 'He even used the clipped dialogue, the fast-paced action and the diamond-hard brilliance of style which became his trademarks.'[4] But the trademarks of these stories are more recognizably those of Jack London and Ring Lardner. Certainly their style is not uniquely Hemingway's; rather, the common 'language of men' is called upon here. Slang, for instance: the protagonists in all these stories speak a non-standard English which is the mark of their separation from a conventional, 'safe' society. It is this same separation, according to Sheridan Baker, which the young Hemingway needed: 'To prove his manhood he must step outside a society that seemed to demand no proof.'[5] Membership in a special male group is stressed, in the boxing story for instance, by the flaunting of that group's slang: 'So I matched the lad with Jim O'Rourke, the old trial horse, and the boy managed to hang one on Jim's jaw that was good for the ten-second anesthetic.' The mature Hemingway will not find it necessary to flaunt his slang to such a degree, even in the stories most like this one, such as 'Fifty Grand'. Yet a certain avoidance of standard English persists, and even more an avoidance of 'literary' English: Grebstein observes that 'Hemingway's most characteristic rhythms are . . . the choppy rhythms of colloquial language rather than the sonorous measures of a latinate high style.'[6] Hemingway himself put it more bluntly to a fellow reporter on the Toronto *Star*. 'Goddam,' he said, 'I hate refinement.'[7]

Considerations like these help account for the style of one of Hemingway's first published works, a vignette originally written as a story for the *Star*.

> Minarets stuck up in the rain out of Adrianople across the mud flats. The carts were jammed for thirty miles along the Karagatch road. Water buffalo and cattle were hauling carts through the mud. No end and no beginning. Just carts loaded with everything they owned. The old men and women, soaked through, walked along keeping the cattle moving. The Maritza was running yellow almost up to the bridge. Carts were jammed solid on the bridge with camels bobbing along through them. Greek cavalry herded along the procession. Women and kids were in the carts crouched with mattresses, mirrors, sewing machines, bundles. There was a woman having a kid with a young girl holding a blanket over her and crying. Scared sick looking at it. It rained all through the evacuation.

Recalling that the original story for the Toronto *Star* had been cabled home, it is tempting to give credit for the prose's distinctive tone to the 'cablese' which encouraged maximum succinctness and impact. However, as Charles Fenton has pointed out,[8] the original cable devoted three paragraphs to the subject rather than one: it used many more adjectives; and it manipulated the reader's emotions more overtly. The revised version introduces 'the choppy rhythms of colloquial speech' and, by implication, the kind of masculine attitude that corresponds to these. There are bitten-off fragments: 'No end and no beginning. Just carts loaded with everything they owned.' Whereas in the cable 'her little daughter looks at her in horror and begins to cry', the revised version has her, colloquially, 'scared sick looking at it'. It is even a 'kid' the woman is having – a choice of words which serves no purpose other than to make us conscious of the writer's toughness. In an even later version, Hemingway thought better of this stance, and the 'kid' became a 'baby'. Still, his original choices clearly reveal his bias towards the language of men.

When this has been said, however, it is not enough. The idea of a masculine bias in itself does not account for the fascination and power of Hemingway's style; nor has justice been done to the complexity of the masculine dynamics underlying that style. For such an understanding we must turn to Hemingway's first published book, *In Our Time*. Here the author's style first emerged with its full power; and the book's content is the best commentary on the forces underlying that style. *In Our Time* is a book of stories interspersed with vignettes, including the one on Adrianople. The mixture, Hemingway wrote to Edmund Wilson, was meant

> to give the picture of the whole between examining it in detail. Like looking with your eyes at something, say a passing coastline, and then looking at it with 15X binoculars. Or rather, maybe, looking at it and then going in and living in it – and then coming out and looking at it again. . . .[9]

In all this, there remains the question of what 'it' is. What are we looking at here? Without assuming any obvious answers (such as 'our time'), let us look again.

The first story, 'Indian Camp', is also the most important one. It introduces the central character of Nick Adams when he is only a boy, and shows him learning the lesson whose consequences are explored throughout the rest of the book. Nick is on a camping trip with his father and uncle. He is awakened in the middle of the night to accompany them when his father, a doctor, is taken to an Indian woman who has been in labour for two days. With perfect efficiency, the doctor does what must be done – we are only informed later that this was a Caesarian operation performed with a pen-knife and no anesthetic. 'Her screams are not important,' his father says to Nick. 'I don't hear them because they are not important.' At this the woman's husband, in the bunk above, rolls over against the wall. When the operation is finally over, the husband is discovered to have slit his throat in despair. This would suggest, at the least, that the woman's screams *were* in fact important, to have affected the husband to such a degree. But Nick is not eager to take the husband's point of view, which after all is what has caused his death. The boy's loyalties remain with his father. He has learned that those who feel emotion die; those who reject it are free to function as a man should.

The story's last sentence shows Nick rejecting not merely death itself but the specific death that is inherent in emotion: 'In the early morning on the lake sitting in the stern of the boat with his father rowing, he felt quite sure that he would never die.' It would be natural to read this sentence as a standard literary irony: that of the *naif* who, given a vision of the darker experience awaiting him later in life, sidesteps it on the grounds that it cannot really apply to him (an example is Mansfield's 'Her First Ball'). But the story and its point are not nearly so standard as that. Its subtleties are clarified if we look at the original story's first few pages – pages which Hemingway finally left out in accordance with his new theory that 'you could omit anything if you knew that you omitted . . . and make people feel something more than they understood.'[10] It was not the unimportant things but the important ones that were usually omitted, so that their presence could be felt without being stated. In this case, the omitted pages tell us several important things. We learn that Nick is not blissfully ignorant of death, but rather is newly aware of it:

> Just a few weeks before at home, in church, they had sung a hymn, 'Some day the silver cord will break.' While they were singing the hymn Nick had realized that some day he must die. It made him feel quite sick. It was the first time he had ever realized that he himself would have to die sometime.[11]

That night he stayed up till morning, afraid to sleep, as he is later to do in the story 'Now I Lay Me'. This night he has been left in camp alone by his father and his Uncle George, who have gone off fishing; and he feels the fear return. He fires off a rifle to call them back. The older men are aware only that Nick's fear is an unmanly thing. 'You don't want to ever be frightened in the woods, Nick,' his father tells him. Uncle George's reaction is less sympathetic: he seems to function throughout the story as a cruder version of the masculine values embodied by Nick's father. He has to be placated:

> 'I know he's an awful coward,' his father said, 'but we're all yellow at that age.'
> 'I can't stand him,' George said. 'He's such an awful liar.'

Nick's tendency to lie connects with his tendency, at the story's end, to lie to himself. That 'he felt quite sure that he would never die' contradicts his earlier knowledge of death; and there has been nothing in the sordid events of the night that would provide a redeeming vision. The remaining possibility is that Nick's statement is a willed assertion, a choice not to die. There is a choice only because his father has offered the alternative of his masculine composure, his rejection of the emotion that seems to lead to death – whether that emotion is pity, despair, or fear itself.

Such a reading of the story is enriched by the pattern of what might be called, echoing Bettelheim, 'symbolic wounds'. There are three such wounds here: there is the 'wound' of the woman's sex; there is the incision of the Caesarian; and there is the husband's cut throat. The Caesarian incision replaces the natural opening of a woman's body to make delivery possible by the male doctor where the woman has failed. The Caesarian is an act of possession, literalizing some of the commonest metaphors for sexual intercourse. A male-determined wound replaces the 'wise wound' of the woman; masculine control replaces awe. This is reflected in the doctor's reaction when he has finished the job: he is 'exalted and talkative as football players are in the dressing room after a game'. Such a male reaction is in contrast to that of the other male in the story. The fathers, the doctor says, are 'usually the worst sufferers in these little affairs'. This is partly because they lack just what produces the doctor's euphoria: the sense of control and practical expertise. Above all they suffer because of emotional identification with their women. The male in this story who cuts his throat has carried that identification to an extreme; he has thereby been womanized. This is not only because a sense of failing as a man usually attaches to suicide in Hemingway. In the imagery of this story all wounds are in one way or another female, even when they are self-inflicted by a male. To be sure, we are not dealing here with a castration that is literal, but the positioning of the wound could not be more significant if it were.

'I must say,' the doctor comments as he moves to check the father, 'he took it all pretty quietly.' The cut throat explains this masculine self-control even as it reverses its significance. It is too much to suggest that the Indian cut his throat to prevent himself from screaming. However, one cannot help wondering what the outcome would have been if he had *not* taken it all 'pretty quietly'. Had the father screamed unabashedly, his emotion might have been 'delivered' naturally through the mouth, and it might not have been necessary to make the 'Caesarian' incision of the throat. Such a release of emotion might have saved his life, though it would have left him no less womanized in his own eyes and society's. Octavio Paz's explanation of reserve in the Mexican *macho* is useful here, particularly for the imagery employed. The *macho*, he tells us, is 'a hermetic being, closed up in himself'. He is invulnerable to the assaults of the outside world and his manliness is measured by that invulnerability. He must always resist the temptation, under adversity or stress, to open up emotionally. Whatever else the outside world may do to him, the *macho* cannot allow it to penetrate his privacy. 'Women,' in this view, 'are inferior beings because, in submitting, they open themselves up.'[12] Whether by screaming or by the wound which silences those screams the Indian too opens himself up. His real mistake is to feel too much to begin with, and to allow those feelings to penetrate and possess him. This is a mistake that Nick's father does not make. And in the end Nick chooses his father's orthodox masculine view over all the others that the story implies are possible.

In Our Time is largely a study of the consequences of Nick's choice and therefore a study of masculine reserve. In 'The Doctor and the Doctor's Wife', for instance, Nick's father backs down from a male face-off between himself and an Indian he has hired to saw logs. The story devotes as much attention to the aftermath of this incident as to the incident itself. It observes what Nick's father does with his undischarged anger, an anger that is most clearly indicated by the vigorous cleaning of his shotgun: 'He pushed the magazine full of the heavy yellow shells and pumped them out again.' His wife offers her own version of the importance of restraining emotion:

> 'Oh,' said his wife. 'I hope you didn't lose your temper, Henry.'
> 'No,' said the Doctor.
> 'Remember, that he who ruleth his spirit is greater than he who taketh a city,' said his wife.

The naïveté of her Christianity, the cloying sweetness of her reiterated 'dear', her extreme sensitivity to light and sound – these colour the wife's version of emotional restraint and make it unpalatable. It is as if feminine notions of restraint were being opposed to masculine ones. Given the alternatives, Nick makes the same choice as in the first story: he chooses to follow his father.

The theme of masculine reserve is most often evident throughout *In Our Time* in the distrust of talking. It is by talking that one opens up to another person and becomes vulnerable. It is by putting words to an emotion that it becomes feminized. As long as the emotion is restrained, held back, it hardly matters what the emotion itself is; it will retain a male integrity. Most explicit on the dangers of talking is the story 'Soldier's Home'. Though the returned soldier is here called Harold Krebs, the story continues the sequence of Nick Adams's experiences; both characters are masks of the young Hemingway. Krebs learns soon enough not to talk about his experiences in the war. His listeners, demanding to be thrilled, have made it impossible for him to hold steadily to the truth. 'Krebs acquired the nausea in regard to experience that is the result of untruth or exaggeration'; he has fallen into easy poses; and 'in this way he lost everything.' What he loses, betrays with words, is the masculine integrity that really was inherent in his experiences. 'All of the times that had been able to make him feel cool and clear inside himself when he thought of them; the times so long back when he had done the one thing, the only thing for a man to do, easily and naturally, now lost their cool valuable quality and then were lost themselves.' Krebs's parents have points of similarity to those in 'The Doctor and the Doctor's Wife'. The mother has the same overt Christianity. In addition – and in contrast to his father, who is 'non-committal' – Krebs's mother is prone to overt emotion:

> 'I'm your mother,' she said. 'I held you next to my heart when you were a tiny baby.'
> Krebs felt sick and vaguely nauseated.

His mother's emotion has bullied him into lying once again, into betraying his true sense of himself. Still he consoles himself with the hope that 'none of it had touched him', and the expectation of his imminent escape.

In these examples, the Doctor's view prevails and the 'stiff upper lip' is by and large a good thing. But there have been from the start other ways of viewing masculine reserve: in 'Indian Camp', after all, *both* men deal with the crisis 'pretty quietly'. That story has established the fundamental ambiguity of masculine reserve. Not talking is a demonstration of masculine control over emotion; but it is also and ultimately self-destructive. When emotion finds no release outwards, it turns inward on its possessor (or possessed). Hemingway expresses this in several stories that criticize the very *macho* values which elsewhere he upholds.

For all Hemingway's aggressive subscription to male values he is aware of the limits of those values; and he incorporates this awareness into the pieces which make up *In Our Time*. Several of the stories even take as their subject the limits of the masculine role. 'The Battler' illustrates Nick Adams's stated credo, 'you got to be tough', with a fighter who *was* tough; but his toughness has profited him nothing in his life and left him dependent on the soft-voiced Bugs, with his refined, courtly diction. 'The End of Something' describes the way Nick breaks off with his girl friend Marjorie. The closest Nick gets to revealing his reasons is his comment, 'You know everything.' A dozen details in the text show that what Marjorie knows a lot about is fishing; and it is apparent that a large part of the tension arises from Nick's incapacity to deal with her 'unfeminine' usurpation of his expertise. It is not surprising, then, that Hemingway can be critical as well of masculine reserve.

'The Three-Day Blow' records a peculiarly male conversation between Nick and his friend Bill. The story scathingly anatomizes their ritualized shallowness, their need to get drunk and subsequent need to demonstrate that they are not drunk, their fetish for practicality, and finally their studious avoidance of the one subject that is charged with emotion and need: Nick's recent break-up with Marjorie. When the subject finally comes to the surface, both Nick and Bill recognize it as a breach of male etiquette.

> 'All of a sudden it was over,' Nick said. 'I oughtn't to talk about it.'
> 'You aren't,' Bill said. 'I talked about it and now I'm through. We won't ever speak about it again. . . .'

The proper male state of mind is that of the three-day blow itself. Upon stepping outdoors, the break-up with Marjorie loses its importance: 'The wind blew it out of his head.' Nick's interior landscape is then left as bare as the exterior landscape described at the story's opening. At that time Nick picks up an apple from the ground, reflecting his desire to preserve a residue of emotion about his relationship with Marjorie. But it is a forbidden fruit that he seeks to have – forbidden by the rules of masculine reserve. The entire story is an illustration of those rules, so much that we may suspect Hemingway of a punning intent in Nick's final comment on the possibility of seeing Marjorie again: 'It was a good thing to have in reserve.'

The full consequences of reserve reveal themselves in a Nick Adams story not included in this book, though it was written at the same time. 'A Way You'll Never Be' shows how a soldier under stress finally snaps. In it Nick pours forth a mad monologue on catching grasshoppers for bait, a pedantic parody of dispassionate observation and practicality. His emotion has undermined the conscious strategy by which he 'noticed everything in such detail to keep it all straight so he would know just where he was'. The source of Nick's emotion has been his full realization that he *can* die, after all: he finds himself observed with familiar masculine practicality by 'the man with the beard who looked at him over the sights of the rifle, quite calmly before squeezing off'. Seeing himself for the first time as the victim of masculine lack of emotion, Nick has nevertheless no way to deal with the emotion aroused by this realization except by the very strategies of detachment which threaten him. This paradoxical circle spins faster and faster, spinning him finally into madness.

Hemingway's most extreme exercise in masculine reserve is the book's closing story, 'Big Two-Hearted River'. It seems at first a perfect illustration of Mailer's point about the masculine fascination with technical surface. We are given all the practical details of Nick's hike to his camping place, the pitching of his tent, the cooking of his evening meal, the catching of grasshoppers for bait, and the strategies of his fishing. These are familiar male rituals, but the excessive attention paid to them hints at obsession, compulsion. Practicality protests too much, and thus betrays the presence of something opposed to it. The source of the implied emotion is the same as that in 'A Way You'll

Never Be'. This is a story, its author said, 'about coming back from the war but there was no mention of the war in it'.[13] 'Big Two-Hearted River' is then an ultimate test of Hemingway's theory of omission. Yet he provides us with ways of sensing the nature of the thing left out. Subtle, half-buried symbols abound. The burned town of Seney and the blackened country around it evoke the ravaged landscape of war. The grasshoppers who have taken on the black colour of their surroundings indicate the effect that similar surroundings may have had on Nick's psychology. In contrast, there is the vision of the trout in the river, 'keeping themselves steady in the current with wavering fins'. Nick, too, is attempting to keep himself steady; and he has a measured consciousness of the limits to his equilibrium. For this reason he does not enter the dark swamp where 'fishing was a tragic adventure'. He will wait for another day to enter its deeper waters. For now, he chooses to stay near the surface of things.

We see the choice made in one of the rare moments when Hemingway gives us an explicit hint of Nick's state: 'His mind was starting to work. He knew he could choke it because he was tired enough.' Alerted by this kind of statement, a reader might well view in more than one light a later statement like 'He did not want to rush his sensations any.' It is not just a matter of relishing and savouring a pleasurable sensation; it is a matter of distrusting any sensation, even that of pleasurable excitement, which threatens to get out of control and deprive Nick of his inner steadiness. Revealing subtleties can be detected even in the choice of individual words. The trout, when Nick first sees them, are judged to be 'very satisfactory' – and later the mosquito he burns up with a lit match 'made a satisfactory hiss in the flame'. 'Satisfactory' is a curious word here. It implies a standard, and a watchful assessment in the light of that standard: Will this measure up? Is this all right? More than a word like 'satisfying' it has an aura of the pedantic, almost the prissy. In fact it is a one-word flicker of the mad monologue in 'A Way You'll Never Be'. Details like these imply an internal warfare in Nick. The shifting front of his private battle is conveyed most of all by shifts in sentence rhythm. Serene, luminous, almost liturgical at one moment, sentences become staccato and nervous the next. The psychological effect of their rhythms is powerful enough to contradict the assurances of the surface:

> Nick was happy as he crawled inside the tent. He had not
> been unhappy all day. This was different though. Now things
> were done. There had been this to do. Now it was done. It had
> been a hard trip. He was very tired. That was done. He had
> made his camp. He was settled. Nothing could touch him.

Whatever Nick's feelings may be, they are not allowed to come to
the surface of his mind, nor to the surface of the page. Only as
Nick sleeps, in the vignette that separates the two halves of 'Big
Two-Hearted River', are we allowed a glimpse of what lies
beneath. The vignette deals with a prisoner condemned to death
who is utterly undone by his fear. The only advice he is given is
'Be a man, my son.'

In Our Time thus closes with yet another story whose subject is
the nature of reserve. Those of its stories not explicitly about
reserve are yet written according to reserve's aesthetic. We are
now in a position to appreciate how complex that aesthetic can
be. For what has been said here about talking applies as well to
writing. The parallel is emphasized by the discarded original
conclusion to 'Big Two-Hearted River', consisting of a kind of
stream-of-consciousness monologue on writing. In it Nick
Adams thinks 'Talking about anything was bad. Writing about
anything actual was bad. It always killed it.' For this reason he
asserts that 'the only writing that was any good was what you
made up, what you imagined.' And he goes on to give a revealing example:

> Of course he'd never seen an Indian woman having a baby.
> That was what made it good. Nobody knew that. He'd seen a
> woman have a baby on the road to Karagatell and tried to help
> her. That was the way it was.

'The way it was': this phrase is one often used by Hemingway to
stress the writer's responsibility to tell the truth. Here, though,
he is admitting that the events of 'Indian Camp' are precisely *not*
the truth, but something much more sensational than what actually happened. The husband's cutting of his throat increases
horror simply by adding to its quantity. The same degree of
horror for the reader could have been obtained without gratuitous lying, by centering on the *quality* of the woman's plight, the
way it was. The throat-cutting episode can only be justified,

then, in the light of a deeper structure of meaning; and I have already suggested that this structure of meaning concerns itself with the nature of reserve. The boy Nick learns the danger of opening one's self up to emotion; and beneath the lies of the surface, the story tells us 'the way it was' for the young Ernest as well.

Hemingway's concern with truth deserves a reassessment in the light of contemporary theories about 'truth' in writing – specifically, those of Jacques Derrida. At a time when writing is often analysed in terms of the relation of signifier to signified, Derrida argues that the signified does not exist, that there is no ultimate 'truth' toward which the signifier points. All writing is a 'trace' or track – but not necessarily the track of a truth, even an unknowable truth. We are signifying beings, but make signifiers only in order to convey still more significations, all of them 'traces' of our own signifying nature. For a writer to talk about his or her relationship to 'truth', then, is always problematical. If the writer is a man, he may well conceive that relationship as similar to another problematical area, his relationship to the woman. Derrida's ideas may be summarized as a gender myth, and have been so summarized by his translator, Gayatri Spivak:

> To possess the woman, one must *be* the woman . . . and yet the being of the woman is unknown. The masculine style of possession through the stylus, the stiletto, the spurs, breaks down as protection against the enigmatic femininity of truth.[14]

The metaphors for writing here are particularly apt to Hemingway. Especially the 'stylus' evolving into the 'stiletto' links the writer's instrument with that of the doctor in 'Indian Camp'. The doctor operates upon the body of a woman in actuality; the writer – if we adopt Derrida's terms – operates upon a woman's body metaphorically. Both are attempting a masculine act of control over that which, to the male mind, symbolizes the enigmatic and unknowable. Both Hemingway and his doctor protagonist withhold themselves from emotional involvement or identification; and to that degree, in Derrida's terms, are unwilling to *be* the woman. Instead of opening themselves up, they attempt to open *her* up, by an incisive style, or stylus, or stiletto.

Above all – and perhaps more than any other style – Hemingway's style is one that gives us the *feeling* of a 'trace'. The beautifully crafted, dispassionate sentences make us more conscious of the signifying function; and at the same time that which is signified withdraws. It is 'the thing left out'. Paradoxically, it makes its presence known by an absence: in Hemingway's words, he will 'make people feel something more than they understood'. To feel more than you understand is the usual condition of life; and in this way Hemingway's stories are 'true to life'. They preserve the way it was and is. Telling, as it is practised in 'Soldier's Home', causes Krebs to lose the way it was. Hemingway's art, in contrast, preserves the truth as such because its telling is never fully attained.

If all this is viewed in terms of masculine and feminine, we are faced with a fundamental ambiguity. Plainly Hemingway's style is in one sense an extension of the masculine values he depicts: the restraint of emotion, the stiff upper lip, the *macho* hermeticism. At the same time, that style preserves in each story a truth that one is made to feel can never be fully known. That quality of truth is one that has already been denominated feminine, eluding as it does any masculine control. Masculine reserve thus modulates imperceptibly into feminine unknowableness. And Hemingway becomes the ostentatiously masculine creator of 'feminine' absences. Approached in such gender-linked terms, the text becomes a tissue of paradox: 'Man and woman change places, exchange their masks to infinity.'[15]

Like many another masculine value, reserve thus turns out to be neither straightforward nor simple – especially in Hemingway's version. Inherent in it is always its own reverse. As subject matter, its ambiguities have been explored throughout *In Our Time*. As style, reserve is plainly fundamental not just to the problematics of Hemingway's writing, but to those of writing in general. And in the writer himself? I have compared Hemingway to the doctor of 'Indian Camp', opening up the body of a feminine truth. But there is the other male in that story who reverses this by opening himself up. He does this, we can be sure, because of emotion – though whether it is to prevent emotion's release or to allow that release is ultimately unknowable. It is just, in the story, the way it was. There is much in Hemingway's life, too, whose true nature is equally unknowable. But it may have been a gesture with some significance that when Hemingway decided to die, he shot himself in the mouth.

CHAPTER 3

The cult of the body

On the morning of 25 November 1970, Yukio Mishima – at the age of forty-five perhaps Japan's best-known writer – rose earlier than usual. He shaved slowly and carefully, knowing that this would be his death face. Before leaving the house, he placed on the hall table an envelope addressed to his publishers; it contained the final instalment of his novel *The Decay of the Angel*. Carrying an old samurai sword, he got into a car with four young students. All of them wore the uniforms of the Tatenokai, a small right-wing militia unit formed by Mishima which was dedicated to the service of the emperor and the restoration of traditional Japanese militarism. The Tatenokai had received training and special privileges from the Japanese army; and it was to one of the large army bases that the car drove now. There they had an appointment with General Mashita, commander of the Eastern Army. The General received them cordially, not really knowing what their business might be. He had just finished admiring Mishima's sword when one of the students throttled him from behind. A gag was stuffed in his mouth, and he was quickly bound to his chair. He was now a hostage. His life would be spared only if Mishima's demands were agreed to. These were: that all the soldiers of the base would be assembled in front of the building; that Mishima would be allowed to make a speech to them from the balcony outside the General's office; and that this speech would be heard in silence and without interruption. After some confusion, the army agreed to these demands.

So it was that at noon precisely Mishima leapt up on the parapet to address a crowd that was, however, far from silent. Soldiers shouted excitedly to each other; ambulances and police cars ran their engines; helicopters buzzed close to film the scene.

Mishima's speech was planned to incite the army to rebellion against the Constitution which, since 1947, forbids Japan to maintain an active army. He had only spoken a few sentences, though, when the first hostile calls began to punctuate the air; and they continued to the end of his speech. Looking down on the crowd, Mishima scornfully said 'I have lost my dream of the army,' and concluded with a triple cry of salute to the emperor. It is unlikely that he ever really believed in the possibility of a spontaneous uprising – only that his plea for one would give meaning to what followed.

Back in the General's office, Mishima, according to plan, prepared for the rite of *seppuku*. He stripped down to a white loincloth and knelt on the carpet. In his hand he held the *yori-doshi*, a sharp foot-long dagger. Behind him stood the student Morita holding Mishima's long samurai sword. His function was to behead Mishima after the suicide; and he would follow him in death shortly after. Tentatively, Mishima touched the tip of the dagger to a point on the lower left side of his abdomen. Once more he shouted the triple salute to the emperor. There was a pause. He drew in his breath, then expelled it all at once in the intense cry characteristic of the Japanese martial arts: and he drove the dagger into his stomach with all his strength. His face went white. The hand on the dagger hilt began to tremble as, back hunched over, Mishima slowly began to make a deep horizontal cut across his stomach from left to right. The white loincloth was now red. As he completed the cut, he toppled forward on his face. Intestines slid from his belly. The shaken Morita slashed with the sword, but hit the dying man's body, not his neck. Only after three tries was Mishima's head separated from his body. The students then knelt and silently said a Buddhist prayer.

Mishima's last action was for him the ultimate realization of manhood. His long journey towards that realization marks him clearly as one of the School of Virility, with significant similarities to the authors we have already considered. The intertwining of art and action which we have seen in Mailer's stabbing of his wife is present in Mishima too. There had been numerous artistic rehearsals for his suicide: the lovingly detailed account of *seppuku* in the story 'Patriotism'; the ardent sacrifice of the young Isao in *Runaway Horses*; and even a film, *The Rite of Love and Death*, in which Mishima himself acted out the ritual disembowelling. That he should be the star of his own film is typical: Mishima had a talent for self-advertisement to rival Mailer's. Like Mailer, he played aggressively masculine roles in films like *The Assassins*, in which he was a terrorist, and *Tough Guy*, in which he was a gangster. To publicize this last movie he was in the habit of opening his shirt for the press, in order to flaunt the hair on his chest. The reminiscence of Hemingway is not surprising, for there are many similarities between the two, both in art and life. As we shall see, reserve is an important part of Mishima's writing style, though it was certainly not present already in boyhood, as it was with Hemingway. Yet the boyhoods of the two men have their similarities.

Mishima's family life seems to have been an extreme version of the split between the sexes depicted in 'The Doctor and the Doctor's Wife'. From the time he was a baby, he was virtually owned by a neurasthenic grandmother; and on her death possession reverted to a no less doting mother, who encouraged her son's literary endeavours. Anything literary was to Mishima's father useless rubbish: he stood for a career in law, Nazism, and the masculine virtues. In John Nathan's biography, the father tells in his own words of one attempt to instil these virtues. Kimitake Hiraoka (Mishima's real name) was only four at the time:

> On one of the many occasions when I had fought with my mother and finally pulled Kimitake away from her and taken him out for a walk, we came to a railroad crossing just as a steam engine was roaring down the tracks toward us belching black smoke and making a terrific racket. There was a fence separating us from the tracks, but the engine passed so close you could touch it if you put out your hand. I thought to myself, Here is a perfect chance for some spartan training. I lifted Kimitake and, shielding his face with my hat, held him out toward the engine and said 'Are you scared? Don't worry – and if you cry like a weakling I'll throw you in a ditch.' As I spoke I looked down at Kimitake's face and was astonished to see there was no reaction. I waited for the next train and tried again, but the result was the same, no effect! Was he like a puppy I wondered, too young to know fear, or had the school-girl training he was getting from my mother made him insensitive to this kind of turbulent, masculine experience? I

felt deflated. The next day I came back and tried with a quieter train. But Kimitake's face was the same Nō mask as before. I gave up. I couldn't solve the riddle.[1]

The attitudes displayed by Mishima's father are as much a riddle as anything else. It is only understandable that the young man shunned his father's way. It is perhaps less understandable that, at about thirty, he began eagerly to follow it, engaging in boxing, judo, karate, kendo, weightlifting and even army training. Like Hemingway and Mailer, Mishima pursued manhood without respite. His ideas on the existential demands of that pursuit sound exactly like those of Mailer: 'To be . . . a man was to be required to give constant proof of one's manliness – to be more of a man today than yesterday, more a man tomorrow than today.'[2]

That Mishima was homosexual does not exclude him from these concerns – nor from the School of Virility, any more than lesbians are excluded from feminist literature. Rather his homosexuality gives an added intensity to the pursuit of manhood; and it may account for the personal rationale that underlay his strenuous physical activities. That rationale was that each workout brought him closer to his goal of becoming a model male object. So far his rationale does not seem very different from that of the weightlifter who checks out his muscles in the mirror. Mishima, though, is not merely trying to improve himself, but to become a completely different self. As homosexual, he is attempting to become something he admires and loves, the male object which he senses as 'other'. That male object seems curiously complete, free of the yearning, doubt, and self-consciousness of Mishima's own self. Subjective elements are to him effeminate, lacking in male completeness. In attempting to become object, then, he is attempting to escape his nature as subject. He wishes to be wholly *en-soi*, in Sartre's terms, rather than *pour-soi*. The aim of his existential endeavour is to eliminate just those aspects of himself which are most existential. To become a man must be finally to attain the solidity and self-containment of an object.

Words would consequently be something to be wary of, because of their connection to the subjective. An object that is self-contained does not have to open itself up in words. So when Mishima is about to relate an incident in which he came close to attaining this state he says, 'It is a rather risky matter to discuss a happiness that has no need of words.'[3] The comment is reminiscent of Hemingway's distrust of talking. But Mishima's relationship with words has a form that is distinctly his own.

> When I examine closely my early childhood, I realise that my memory of words reaches back far farther than my memory of the flesh. In the average person, I imagine, the body precedes language. In my case, words came first of all; then – belatedly, with every appearance of extreme reluctance, and already clothed in concepts – came the flesh. It was already, as goes without saying, sadly wasted by words.
>
> First comes the pillar of plain wood, then the white ants that feed on it. But for me, the white ants were there from the start, and the pillar of plain wood emerged tardily, already half eaten away.[4]

The comparison to white ants is made on the basis of what Mishima calls the 'corrosive function' of words. Applied to any object, they eat into it with all their powers of subjectivity. One as immersed in words as Mishima cannot even see an external reality any more, but only the words for it. It is this state from which he longs to escape: 'Oh, the fierce longing simply to see, without words!'[5] Words and seeing are woven together inextricably. For this reason an analysis of Mishima's ideas on the act of seeing will by implication also tell us much about his attitude towards words.

Seeing is a recurrent preoccupation in Mishima's work; and this act of seeing may either have others as its object, or it may be directed at one's self. Seeing others is most dramatically rendered by the many cases of voyeurism in Mishima's works. One such case is Honda in the tetralogy entitled *The Sea of Fertility*. In the third book Honda uses a peephole in the adjoining bedroom to spy on Ying Chan, a young woman with whom he is obsessed, in a way reminiscent of a similar scene in *The Sailor Who Fell From Grace with the Sea*. In the last book he has become a confirmed voyeur, at seventy-six lurking in the shadows of the park at night to watch young couples on the grass. At the same time we are told that 'the evil suffusing [Honda's] life had been self-awareness.'[6] Self-awareness, the continual seeing of one's self, is only another version of the subjective function that seeing represents. Honda's nature as a man who continually sees – whether himself or others – is brought out by what is said of Tōru, a sixteen-year-old boy whom Honda immediately recognizes as his perfect psychological duplicate. Tōru is completely self-aware:

> He knew his workings to their smallest parts. His inspection system was flawless. There was no unconscious.
>   'If I had ever spoken or moved from the smallest sub-conscious impulse, then the world would have been promptly destroyed. The world should be grateful for my awareness of myself. . . .'[7]

Tōru's clear psychological vision of himself is matched by the sharpness of his physical vision. His job is to watch the sea from a signal tower and to notify the harbour officials of the impending arrival of ships. He experiences 'the happiness of watching' to the furthest limits; and here too his clarity is inhuman. He knows that 'no eye could be clearer or brighter than the eye that had nothing to create, nothing to do but gaze.' And he wishes to extend that gaze even to the point that it is purified of anything like an object. He imagines

> a sea never defiled by being, a sea upon which ships never appeared. There had to be a realm where at the limit of all the layers of clarity it was definite that nothing at all made an appearance, a realm of solid, definite indigo, where seeing cast off the shackles of consciousness and itself became transparent, where phenomena and consciousness dissolved like plumbic oxide in acetic acid.[8]

It is significant that in Tōru's extreme version of seeing he desires not only to annihilate the object but also the subject. His desire to 'cast off the shackles of consciousness' can apply equally to the physical act of seeing and to psychological self-awareness. Both forms of seeing have in Tōru been pushed to the point of their own destruction.

In the fourth book of the tetralogy we witness Tōru's destruction. Tōru learns that there is unmistakable evidence of his being the third reincarnation of Honda's boyhood friend Kiyoaki, who died for love at the age of twenty. Every other incarnation has also died at twenty; and as his birthday nears, Tōru tries to kill himself by taking poison. His motive is left unclear, but it is most likely the discovery that his self-awareness is not as comprehensive as he has thought it was when he gave it the power to define his whole life. The suicide attempt fails. Tōru's twentieth birthday passes, and he slowly recovers – only the effects of the poison have cost him his eyesight. He is condemned not to death or reincarnation but to *The Decay of the Angel*, in the words of the book's title. According to Buddhist theology, there are five signs of an angel's final decay, among which is 'loss of self-awareness'. Tōru's self-awareness, when pursued to its conclusion, has led to its own loss and Tōru's decay. 'Immediately at the end of knowledge comes leprosy,' Honda has said earlier.[9] It is himself he is talking about; and Tōru's decay is merely the open manifestation of the spiritual decadence the two have always had in common.

Decay is one way in which seeing, when pushed to its limits, naturally ends in its own destruction. Another way is the way of denial – a willed destruction by the self of the self's compulsive seeing. Honda feels that his voyeurism contaminates Ying Chan; the very act of seeing her binds her to his own limited perceptions.

> It now became clear that Honda's ultimate desire, what he really, really wanted to see could exist only in a world where he did not. In order to see what he truly wished to, he must die. When a voyeur recognizes that he can realize his ends only by eliminating the basic act of watching, this means his death as such.[10]

Tōru, too, aspires to a vision beyond his seeing self, as indicated in a selection from his journal: 'What is it to see the invisible? That is the ultimate vision, the denial at the end of all seeing, the eye's denial of itself.'[11] We have already noted his conscious desire to shed consciousness and escape into 'a realm of solid, definite indigo'. Though in context this seems to refer to sea, it is sky that is in Mishima's mind here – specifically 'the strangely blue sky overhead said to occur at the moment of death'.[12] This solid, intensely blue sky appears again and again in Mishima's work. It is a private symbol whose origin is related in *Sun and Steel*:

> When I was small, I would watch the young men parade the portable shrine through the streets at the local shrine festival.

They were intoxicated with their task, and their expressions were of an indescribable abandon, their faces averted; some of them even rested the backs of their necks against the shafts of the shrine they shouldered, so that their eyes gazed up at the heavens. And my mind was much troubled by the riddle of what it was that those eyes reflected.

. . . It was only much later, after I had begun to learn the language of the flesh, that I undertook to help in shouldering a portable shrine, and was at last able to solve the puzzle that had plagued me since infancy. They were simply looking at the sky. In their eyes there was no vision: only the reflection of the blue and absolute skies of early autumn.[13]

The young men have succeeded in denying the act of seeing ('In their eyes there was no vision') and have momentarily attained a state of pure objectivity, purged of self.

It is not only important that the outside world be pure untainted object; the seer himself must be freed from self-awareness to the point that he too becomes an object. He must become free from the corrosion of subjectivity in order to become wholly beautiful. 'In nature there's no blemish but the mind,' Antonio claims in *Twelfth Night* (III, iv, 401); and for Mishima too, all ugliness is represented by thought. 'It is not allowed to know and still be beautiful,' says Honda;[14] and the statement explains an episode in Mishima's youth related in his autobiographical novel *Confessions of a Mask*. As a schoolboy he developed an intense crush on Omi, a boy who was his direct opposite: mentally slow and non-intellectual, but physically mature and well-built. The most curious thing about this relationship is the way young Mishima makes Omi wholly into a physical object. Instead of hoping to get to know Omi better, instead of looking forward to an exchange of intimate thoughts and feelings, Mishima resists the slightest move in such a direction.

There were times when a whim would bring him peering into the books, erudite and far beyond my years, that I was reading. I would almost always give him a noncommittal smile and close whatever book I was holding, to keep him from seeing it. It was not out of shame: rather, I was pained by any indication that he might have an interest in such things as books, might reveal an awkwardness about them, might seem to weary of his own unconscious perfection.[15]

Mishima's love of Omi's perfection eventually turns into jealousy, and after that to the desire to *become* Omi – to make himself wholly physical, wholly an object, and therefore wholly beautiful. The full story of that endeavour, with its complex shifts and evolutions, is told in *Sun and Steel*. The 'sun' of the title tans his skin, which before had the pallor of those who sink themselves in introversion and night. The 'steel' is that of the weights against which he pits his body, slowly building muscles that are their match. In strenuous physical activity Mishima is able to find fleeing moments of self-forgetfulness; he sees in the same direct and unconscious way as did the shrine bearers years before. Simultaneously, his physical activity is helping his body evolve towards the state of being a pure object, with no external signs of the subjective and individual. 'I had always felt that such signs of physical individuality as a bulging belly (sign of spiritual sloth) or a flat chest with protruding ribs (sign of an unduly nervous sensibility) were excessively ugly,' Mishima tells us. Consequently 'if the body could achieve perfect, non-individual harmony, then it would be possible to shut individuality up forever in close confinement.'[16] This 'perfect, non-individual harmony' is equivalent to the perfect build. Only in such a build can the body fully reveal the power of its own nature, without any modifications or corruptions by the individual sensibility. A similar idea is implied by referring to someone as 'in shape'. Shape is form; and the form of fit male bodies tends remarkably towards the same clear shape: muscled shoulders, deep chest, tapering waist and so on. The body is anonymous, purged of any elements that bespeak individual quirks. Subjectivity is no longer detectable in it; the body approaches the status of pure object, and therefore of beauty.

Once attained, however, the body's beauty as an object has its own perils. For in *Sun and Steel* we are told that 'a strict rule is imposed where men are concerned. It is this: a man must under normal circumstances never permit his own objectivization. . .'[17] Mishima is thinking of those men who exist merely as sexual objects. Beauty in the male, when it becomes an object in itself rather than an almost unconscious by-product, is despised as feminine. This accounts for our impulse to smile at body builders who keep assessing their triceps and pectorals in the gym's mirrors. These virile specimens fall into the actions of clichéd womanhood; thus their virility is comically undermined. Mishima realized the contradiction between the virile object he desired to become and the feminine quality of that desire itself. He had originally hoped that the power of the body would cover its tracks, so to speak, would wipe out the feminine preoccupations that had made him develop his body to begin with. 'In this way,' he tells us, 'my body, while itself the product of an idea, would doubtless also serve as the best cloak with which to hide the idea.'[18] This turned out not to be the case, at least not entirely. Mishima began to feel that the only true way a man could objectify himself was by death.

'You must realize that a man's determination to become a beautiful person is very different from the same desire in a woman; in a man it is always the desire for *death*.'[19] A character in *Kyoko's House* is here voicing Mishima's own opinion. He arrived at this opinion by more than one route. First is the notion that the male body is effeminate if its beauty is without purpose. And the musculature of the body indicates clearly that its purpose is that of the warrior: Perse in *Seamarks* sings the praise of the male body that 'stripped, still shows the marks of armor'. A warrior's purpose is to fulfil himself wherever death is thickest. So Mishima came to the belief that a man's body never shows itself as 'existence'; rather it is a form of existence that rejects existence, and this is 'universal in the male'.[20] At the same time his experiences in karate and kendo were leading him to a fascination with 'that which lurked beyond the flash of the fist and the stroke of the fencing sword', a reality which he felt was 'at the opposite pole from verbal expression'. This reality was the opponent. The opponent, unlike the usual reality which is co-opted and corroded by the act of seeing, gazes back at you. The gaze itself defines you as an object, even before the blow arrives to ratify that definition. For Mishima, this is an entirely new kind of reality. 'Ideas do not stare back; things do. . . . Beyond action, one may glimpse, flitting behind the semitransparent space it has achieved (the opponent) the "thing". To the man of action, that "thing" appears as death, which bears down on him – the great black bull of the toreador – without any agency of the imagination.'[21] As Mishima turned himself into a man of action he became increasingly addicted to the athletic combat, seeing in each combat an imitation of death.

The mere imitation of death, however, could not realize the ultimate purpose of the muscled body; nor could it realize that other intimately linked purpose, to purge the self of self-awareness and to become wholly a masculine object. The forgetfulness of self achieved in mock combats was only momentary: Mishima's self-awareness always returned. And when it did, he could not really be aware of himself as a being who had achieved objectivization. Indeed it is impossible to know that one has attained the state of being an unconsciously masculine object; for in the instant of knowing one is no longer in that state. Only one instant is the exception to this; the instant of actual death.

In *Sun and Steel* Mishima explores this paradox by using the metaphor of an apple. The self-knowledge of the man of letters he sees as a most peculiar fruit: 'a transparent apple whose core is fully visible from the outside'. Such a man is wholly subjective. The objective existence of his body is nothing to him, and so 'transparent'. Virginia Woolf too, in her essay 'On Being Ill', finds that the body in literature is usually a mere transparent vessel for holding emotions and thoughts. These subjective elements are fully visible in literature – and, Mishima would argue, in the life of the man of letters. Because his core is a subjective one, it is accessible to him through his self-awareness and can be endorsed by words. The case is much more complicated in the case of an ordinary apple. It is red and healthy; its flesh is firm and opaque; only the glossy surface is visible from the outside.

> The inside of the apple is naturally quite invisible. Thus at the heart of that apple, shut up within the flesh of the fruit, the core lurks in its wan darkness, tremblingly anxious to find some way to reassure itself that it is a perfect apple. The apple certainly exists, but to the core this existence as yet seems inadequate; if words cannot endorse it, then the only way to endorse it is with the eyes. Indeed, for the core the only sure mode of existence is to exist and to see at the same time. There is only one method of solving this contradiction. It is for a knife to be plunged deep into the apple so that it is split open and the core is exposed to the light – to the same light,

that is, as the surface skin. Yet then the existence of the cut apple falls into fragments; the core of the apple sacrifices existence for the sake of seeing.[22]

Somewhat later the apple metaphor, which has become rather strained, is dropped for a more forthright statement of what is involved:

> . . . the muscles start working in accordance with the demands of self-awareness; but in order to make the action exist unequivocally, a hypothetical enemy outside the muscles is necessary, and for the hypothetical enemy to make certain of its existence it must deal a blow to the realm of the senses fierce enough to silence the querulous complaints of self-awareness. That, precisely, is when the knife of the foe must come cutting into the flesh of the apple – or rather, the body. Blood flows, existence is destroyed, and the shattered senses give existence as a whole its first endorsement, closing the logical gap between seeing and existing. . . . And this is death.[23]

In Mishima's own death, then, we see the resolution of the paradox that obsessed him: how to have knowledge of one's self as wholly an object. Until he became wholly an object he could not feel that he was wholly a man; and to become a man was the existential aim of his life. Only at the moment of death could he achieve that aim and simultaneously know that he had achieved it.

While he was pursuing these ideas, Mishima was continuing to write at least six hours a night. His preoccupation with words and his preoccupation with the muscled body began to affect each other in a curious series of evolutions. At the beginning the body's attraction was that it seemed to be the opposite of words. Its characteristics to Mishima were 'taciturnity and beauty of form'.[24] It may seem surprising that beauty of form should be considered a characteristic opposed to those of literature. This gives us some idea of the extreme degree to which Mishima held the notion of words as fundamentally corrosive. Words dissolve the objective forms of reality in the acid of their own subjectivity. Form may be reconstituted, but only in terms of the verbal, not the real. Literature may imitate the formal beauty of the body, but it can never attain it, because of the inherently corrosive nature of words. Another point of opposition is that the body's formal beauty is always anonymous and universal. One leaves behind individual oddities of form to the degree that one is 'in shape'. In literature the reverse is the case:

> At first, in much the same way as stone coinage, words become current among the members of a race as a universal means to the communication of emotions and needs. As long as they remain unsoiled by handling, they are common property, and they can, accordingly, express nothing but commonly shared emotions.
>
> However, as words become particularized, and as men begin – in however small a way – to use them in personal, arbitrary ways, so their transformation into art begins.[25]

This transformation ends in the glorification of individual literary style.

To rediscover the universal in the verbal, we must move away from artful literary style towards stereotypes and clichés. Only there do we find words without individuality. For this reason Mishima was fascinated by such words – especially when they seemed to emerge spontaneously from the world of the body. Reading a collection of last letters written by young *kamikaze* pilots, he is struck by their stereotyped quality:

> [These letters,] with their pithy phrases about duty to one's fatherland, destroying the enemy, eternal right, and the identity of life and death, obviously selected what were considered to be the most impressive, the most noble from among a large number of ready-made concepts, and clearly revealed a determination, by eliminating anything in the way of personal psychology, to identify the self with the splendid words chosen. . . .
>
> Once there were such words, though they are lost to us nowadays. They were not simply beautiful phrases, but a constant summons to superhuman behavior, words that demanded that the individual stake his very life on the attempt to climb to their own lofty heights. . . .
>
> Their very impersonality and monumentality demanded the strict elimination of individuality and spurned the

construction of monuments based on personal action. . . .
Unlike the words of a genius, the words of a hero must be
selected as the most impressive and noble from among ready-
made concepts. And at the same time they, more than any
other words, constitute a splendid language of the flesh.[26]

A reconciliation of opposites might then be possible; language
and flesh might meet. But for Mishima this could only be in the
most carefully wrought of styles, a style which paradoxically
would seek to eliminate any trace of individual literary style.
Especially he distrusted the 'feminine' inroads of the imagination:

There was no telling when the sickly forces of an invisible
imagination, still lying in wait, might launch their cowardly
assault from without the carefully arrayed fortifications of
style. Day and night, I stood guard on the ramparts. . . . As
guard and weapon against imagination and its henchman
sensibility, I had style. The tension of the all-night watch,
whether by land or by sea, was what I sought after in my style.
More than anything, I detested defeat. Can there be any worse
defeat than when one is corroded and seared from within by
the acid secretions of sensibility until finally one loses one's
outline, dissolves, liquefies. . . ?[27]

The opposite of such a loss of one's outline is the beauty of form
represented by the body. The muscled body then becomes more
and more explicitly the model for Mishima's evolving style:

By now, I had made of my style something appropriate to my
muscles: it had become flexible and free; all fatty
embellishment had been stripped from it, while 'muscular'
ornament – ornament, that is, that though possibly without
use in modern civilization was still as necessary as ever for
purposes of prestige and presentability – had been
assiduously maintained.[28]

The body's posture and pace have their correspondences in
Mishima's new style:

Abounding in antitheses, clothed in an old-fashioned weighty
solemnity, it did not lack nobility of a kind; but it maintained
the same ceremonial, grave pace wherever it went, marching

through other people's bedrooms with precisely the same
tread as elsewhere. Like some military gentleman, it went
about with chest out and shoulders back, despising other
men's styles for the way they stooped, sagged at the knees,
even – heaven forbid! – swayed at the hips.[29]

The most paradoxical correspondence is that between the body's
characteristic of taciturnity and its equivalent in style. Words are
used in such a way as to reject the verbal, thus denying their own
function: 'Just as my body was isolated, so my style was on the
verge of non-communication; it was a style that did not accept,
but rejected.'[30]

So by conscious work parallels might be created even between
two things as opposite in nature as body and words. As time
went by, however, Mishima began to feel that there were actual
and innate parallels between the two. He began to feel, to begin
with, 'that the body's special qualities did not lie solely in taciturnity and beauty of form, but that the body too might have its
own loquacity.'[31] This is a 'language of the flesh', but the phrase
means something different now. Before, it referred to language
which sought to capture and imitate the qualities of the body.
Now the idea is that the body in a sense speaks its own language,
or at any rate has characteristics in common with those of
language. One such characteristic for Mishima is a certain
abstract quality: 'Muscles, of which non-communication is the
very essence, ought never in theory to acquire the abstract quality
common to means of communication. And yet . . .' Mishima
then counters theory with personal experience:

> One summer day, heated by training, I was cooling my
> muscles in the breeze coming through an open window. The
> sweat vanished as though by magic, and coolness passed over
> the surface of the muscles like a touch of menthol. The next
> instant, I was rid of the sense of the muscles' existence, and –
> in the same way that words, by their abstract functioning, can
> grind up the concrete world so that the words themselves
> seem never to have existed – my muscles at that moment
> crushed something within my being, so that it was as though
> the muscles themselves had similarly never existed.[32]

The abstract quality Mishima finds in muscles and words alike is a 'transparent sense of power' – transparent because it necessarily involves the annihilation of its medium. The male body has earlier been described as a paradox, a form of existence that rejects existence. Now we find that words can have a similar quality. 'I had already seen, in the paradox enacted by the body, the ultimate form of the freedom that comes through literature,' Mishima says, 'the freedom that comes through words.'[33] This freedom for both body and words has to do with the rejection of existence, with a constant awareness of the end.

This kind of freedom was never so intense as during the war, which seemed to be the very apotheosis of 'the end'. Even for a civilian like the young Mishima, every instant was fraught with the oncoming destruction. When the war ended, he suffered a tremendous spiritual collapse; he had lost his freedom and had been condemned to life. What he now wanted was to recapture that sense of an ending through the deliberate strategies of his writing:

> . . . my technique in dealing with words was sufficiently practiced for me to choose impersonal words, thereby enhancing their function as a memorial and putting an end to life of my own free will. This – it would be no exaggeration to say – was the only revenge I could take on the spirit of stubbornly refusing to perceive the 'end.' . . .
>
> Somehow or other, I must make my spirit conscious once more of the 'end.' Everything started from there; only there, it was clear, could I find a basis for true freedom.[34]

Deliberate strategies may be used to heighten the power of words to put an end to life, including their own life. However, it is an innate characteristic of all words for Mishima that they have the power to bring to an end – paradoxically, to bring to an end again and again. For they work upon that which has no end in itself: Mishima calls it 'the void in the present progressive tense'.

> This void of the progressive, that may go on for ever while one waits for an absolute that may never come, is the true canvas on which words are painted. This can happen, moreover, because words, in marking the void, dye it as irrevocably as the gay colors and designs on Yuzen fabrics are fixed once they are rinsed in the clear waters of Kyoto's river, and in doing so

consume the void completely moment by moment, becoming fixed in each instant, where they remain. Words are over as soon as they are spoken, as soon as they are written. Through the accumulation of these 'endings,' through the moment-to-moment rupture of life's sense of continuity, words acquire a certain power. . . . And in exchange for the way in which, by marking off each moment, they ceaselessly chop up life's sense of continuity, they act in a way that seems at least to translate the void into substance of a kind.[35]

In this passage, the power of words to end is not much different from their power to create. Both are activities that work upon the surface of the void. This concept is related to the Buddhist philosophy that provides the underpinnings for the whole of *The Sea of Fertility*. In the third book of the tetralogy, *The Temple of Dawn*, we are told that there are three things that cause the world of illusion to materialize. The first of these is 'name' – that is, words which cause things to endure in the memory as concepts. But the sense that these things do endure is an illusion. The world is made up of continual beginnings and endings; every instant has its death and rebirth: 'Samsara and reincarnation are not prepared during a lifetime, beginning only at death, but rather they renew the world at every instant by momentary re-creation and destruction.'[36] This sentence is a pivotal one for the tetralogy. *The Sea of Fertility* has seemed to be a study of reincarnation. Of the two boyhood friends, Kiyoaki is reincarnated every twenty years – as Isao, as Ying Chan, as Tōru; Honda lives on to reach eighty. Yet Honda and Tōru are perfect parallels to one another, for Honda's nature has also gone through its deaths and rebirths; and even this plodding, conservative lawyer has lived many lives in his lifetime. Furthermore, death and reincarnation may be seen to characterize not only a lifetime, nor only certain cycles within a lifetime, but every moment of every life. Tōru with his sharp vision catches a physical glimpse of this truth. It is, as usual, the sea that he is watching at the time. The waves ceaselessly rolling inward seem to him, even as they are created, to be 'mouths agape at the moment of death'. Then he sees something that is not mere metaphor:

He suddenly felt that a different world was being dragged forth from these gaping jaws. Since he was not one to see phantasms, there could be no doubt that it existed. But he did not know what it was. Perhaps it was a pattern drawn by micro-organisms in the sea. A different world was revealed in the light flashing from the dark depths, and he knew it was a place he had seen. Perhaps it had something to do with immeasurably distant memories. If there was such a thing as a previous life, then perhaps this was it. And what would its relation be to the world Tōru was constantly looking for, a step beyond the bright horizon? If it was a dance of seaweed caught in the belly of the breaking waves, then perhaps the world pictured in that instant was a miniature of the mucous pink and purple creases and cavities of the nauseous depths. But there had been rays and flashes – from a sea run through by lightning? Such a thing was not probable in this tranquil twilight sea. There was nothing demanding that *that* world and *this* world be contemporary. Was the world he had had a glimpse of in a different time? Was it of a time different from that measured by his watch?[37]

The answer to these questions must be in the affirmative. Tōru has undoubtedly had a glimpse of one of his own previous incarnations. That incarnation and the momentary incarnation of the wave are superimposed – not just visually, but philosophically. A lifetime and an instant are equally an illusion; distinctions in time are themselves illusions.

It follows that the whole long chronology of *The Sea of Fertility* is also an exercise in illusion. This is fully made clear only in the last pages of the last volume. Honda has been diagnosed to have cancer, and knows that he will die of it. At last he feels able to do something he has not had the courage to do all his life: he journeys to the Buddhist nunnery where Satoko, Kiyoaki's lover, has shut herself up at the conclusion of their affair. She is now the Abbess, aged but still beautiful, and filled with a transcendent holiness. She remembers the outside world well until Honda mentions Kiyoaki's name. Then – 'Kiyoaki Matsugae. Who might he have been?' Even when Honda recounts the story of her love affair with Kiyoaki, Satoko is convinced that she has never known him. Apparently in complete sincerity she suggests that perhaps such a person never existed, for

'Memory is like a phantom mirror. It sometimes shows

things too distant to be seen, and sometimes it shows them as if they were here.'

'But if there was no Kiyoaki from the beginning –' Honda was groping through a fog. His meeting here with the Abbess seemed half a dream. He spoke loudly, as if to retrieve the self that receded like traces of breath vanishing from a lacquer tray. 'If there was no Kiyoaki, then there was no Isao. There was no Ying Chan, and who knows, perhaps there has been no I.'

For the first time there was strength in her eyes.

'That too is as it is in each heart.'

The visit concludes as Honda is shown the garden:

It was a bright, quiet garden, without striking features. Like a rosary rubbed between the hands, the shrilling of cicadas held sway.

There was no other sound. The garden was empty. He had come, thought Honda, to a place that had no memories, nothing.

The noontide sun of summer flowed over the still garden.

This is the close of the whole tetralogy. Like the garden, it is revealed as a study in emptiness. The words have created, momentarily, a beautiful illusion over the void. In the end, *The Sea of Fertility*, whose title promises all the richness of this world, evokes only what Mishima had in mind behind that promise: the barren landscape of the moon.

Its author closes *The Sea of Fertility* with the old format of writing 'The End'. In the context, this has a new and grim significance reinforced by the only words that follow: 25 November 1970, the date of Mishima's death. The end of his tetralogy is intimately connected with his own end – not, however, by way of the Buddhist theory he has presented at such length. That elaborate theory, like his patriotism, is a rationale for what already exists. More deeply rooted than god or country is Mishima's devotion to a masculine ideal. It is not quiescent Buddhist acceptance that attracts him, but an idea of action that is specifically male. Mishima thought of his life as divided into four 'rivers', of which one was the river of action. 'To be a man,' he said, 'is to find this river irresistible.'[38] Virile action, by what Mishima considered a natural progression, leads in the end to death. The river of action, like all the rivers of his life, empties into the 'Sea of Fertility', and is absorbed again by the void. This is also true of his art. As a character in the third book of the tetralogy puts it, 'The arts predict the greatest vision of the end. Before anything else they prepare for and embody the end.'[39]

Yet it is only the end that unites art and action. Until the end, they seem to be irreconcilable.

> To be utterly familiar with the essence of these two things – of which one must be false if the other is true – and to know completely their sources and partake of their mysteries, is secretly to destroy the ultimate dreams of one concerning the other.
>
> . . . the dual approach cuts one off from all salvation by dreams: the two secrets that should never by rights have been brought face to face see through each other. Within one body, and without flinching, the collapse of the ultimate principles of life and of death must be accepted.[40]

So writes Mishima in *Sun and Steel*. A 'dual way of the pen and sword' is, of course, part of the samurai tradition that Mishima admires: the samurai should be able to write a poem and cut down an enemy with equal grace and strength. Mishima, however, is a man of his time in finding a fundamental contradiction between the two. 'It is one thing to talk of the dual way of the pen and the sword,' he says, 'but the true merger can be achieved only in the instant of death.'[41] Mishima achieved that merger, resolving in the only possible way the paradoxes that troubled his sense of masculinity. For one instant, he was a man.

CHAPTER 4

The pen and the penis

To pursue the body with words is a hard task for any writer. It is made harder by the fact that the body, of all things, is most difficult to see steadily and to see whole. Margaret Walters's book on *The Male Nude* has recently made us aware that a man's body, as much as a woman's, may be reinterpreted according to the vision of each era.[1] There is little steadiness to be found in these visions of the body; nor do we all that often see the body whole. This emerges most clearly in the extreme case of erotic and pornographic literature, which is commonly a wild assemblage of cocks, cunts, mouths and buttocks – an art of parts. But even perfectly respectable people not given to erotic excess will give prominence to one part or another; and this may not be a matter of personal taste, but of a social one. Each era discovers, as if for the first time, the existence of some part of the body. Privately, of course, one always knows that these parts exist. But it is the social recognition of these parts that is of interest, their introduction into art and literature as things that may now be spoken of and looked at directly. Discovering is often paralleled by *un*covering of the part in question, or at least its accentuation by clothing styles. An example is the Victorian discovery of the bosom. In our time there are good indications that the part in question is the penis.

The advent of beefcake magazines for women, such as *Playgirl*, has introduced photographs of the male genitals into the 'image bank' of respectable society. The organs flaunted in these glossy pages are glamourized by a policy which has been summed up as 'maximum tumescence in repose'.[2] Still, they are real in the sense that they are not the terrible 'weapons' of De Sade or the 'engines' of Cleland, but obviously and unblushingly flesh. It seems that the fig leaf of metaphor has finally dropped. When there is a covering, it is a new covering which has evolved more or less humorously: the so-called 'cock sock', for instance, and a pair of trousers designed by Eldridge Cleaver which incorporate a kind of elongated codpiece. The gesture has a certain significance. For pants are in themselves asexual, and could only be considered especially male in añ era when women were supposed to have no nether limbs. The new emphasis on the penis has even raised it from the status of an object to that of a character: the penis of the leading man plays a leading role in Marco Ferreri's recent film, *The Last Woman*. It is, for the first time outside pornography, shown erect; it is addressed as if it were another person; and at the film's end relations between the penis and its owner are severed with an electric carving knife.

This last example introduces psychological dimensions which are the most interesting aspects of the new trend. What is being investigated – perhaps for the first time – is a man's relationship to that part which defines him as a man. Phenomenologists, who have explored the perception of one's own hand and foot and eye, have been oddly demure where this part is concerned. Yet more than any other bodily part, the penis has a disconcerting tendency to independence. Leonardo da Vinci, in one of his notebooks, observes that this part of the body

> has intelligence of itself, and although the will of the man desires to stimulate it, it remains obstinate and takes its own course, and moving sometimes of itself without licence or thought by the man, whether he be sleeping or waking, it does what it desires; and often the man is asleep and it is awake, and many times the man is awake, and it is asleep.[3]

It is this tendency to independence that Connie becomes aware of in *Lady Chatterley's Lover*:

> Vaguely, she realised for the first time in her life what the phallus meant, and her heart seemed to enter a new, wide world. Between the two hesitating, baffled creatures, himself and her, she had seen the third creature, erect, alert, overweening, utterly unhesitating, stand there in a queer new assertion, rising from the roots of his body. It was like some primitive, grotesque god: but alive, and unspeakably vivid,

alert with its own weird life, apart from both their personalities. Sightless, it seemed to look round, like a mole risen from the depths of the earth. The resurrection of the flesh, it was called in joke. But wasn't it really so? Wasn't there a weird, grotesque godhead in it?[4]

Through Connie, Lawrence goes on to talk about the modern fear of 'this *alter ego*, this homunculus, this little master which is inside a man, the phallus. Men and women alike committed endless obscenities in order to be rid of this little master, to be free of it!'

These last observations sum up the general plot of two works of the 1970s which centre around the penis. The best-known of these is *Portnoy's Complaint*, about which much has already been written. '*Ven der putz shteht, ligt der sechel im drerd,*' says Portnoy's Yiddish wisdom: 'when the prick stands up, the head goes to hell.' Of course, Portnoy uses his *putz* as a battering ram to break through the complexities of his Jewishness. From another point of view, though, it uses *him* – drags him through life protesting (excessively) against its excesses. He argues with it; it argues back. Invariably it wins. So thoroughly does every impulse of his penis become acted out that the unhappy man attached to it can complain, 'I have a life *without* latent content.'[5]

This is also the complaint of Alberto Moravia's narrator in *Io et Lui*, translated into English as *The Two of Us*. Rico, at thirty-five, is a hack writer of film scripts who aspires to create a work of art and at the same time make a political statement. If he were sexually sublimated in the standard Freudian sense, all his energies, he feels, would go toward the realization of that goal. Instead, he is 'desublimated': his penis arrogates all energies to itself. Not only is that part of enormous size and overweening activity; it also talks to him. Indeed, it has the status of an independent actor in this novel. In one of Rico's dreams – not so readily distinguishable from his reality – his penis quite literally achieves complete independence:

> . . . I saw him sitting in the armchair at the foot of the bed. He was obviously in a state of exaltation, judging, at least, by his bulk; but at the same time there was nothing exaggerated or unseemly in his attitude. He was sitting upright in the armchair in an urbane, well-bred manner, his head thrown back against the back of the chair, with an air of cheerful

satisfaction like someone who has consumed plenty of good food and drink. A big dark vein, encircling him below his head in the manner of a necktie, even gave the impression that he was dressed. In any case, the darkness which filled the room prevented me from distinguishing details. I could divine, in general, the outlines of his figure, which evoked, strangely, the image of a great octopus with a conical hood squatting upon its own tentacles.[6]

As with any more conventional actor in a novel, his character is analysed at great length. From Rico's point of view,

'he' is no psychologist, has no intuition, in fact, frankly, is not intelligent; and therefore he never understands when certain things can be done and when they can't. It's not by mere chance that, in common parlance, he is often mentioned as the symbol of a certain type of stupidity.[7]

From 'his' own point of view, however, he is not to be seen as 'a mere part of your body, not so different, after all, from your hand or your ear or your nose, but as a god. . .'[8] Incarnated under many names and guises, he is a universal presence, the source of all that is in the world.[9] The problem is how the individual is to live his daily life joined to this creature that is beyond the individual, indeed beyond the human. It pushes Rico towards acts of exhibitionism, voyeurism, sadism, masochism, homosexuality, fetishism – in short, a fairly normal sex life, even if it is reported by Rico in an exaggerated, hysterical style. So familiar to the male reader is this tumultuous relationship with one's own penis that he accepts even the prolonged arguments between the two main characters. The talking penis seems merely a literary convention to convey the tensions between the normal male and his sexual organ. It comes as a surprise, then, well into the novel, to realize that Rico is *not* normal – that he really and truly does hear a voice coming from his own penis. This is made plain during a brief visit to a psychoanalyst friend, which also indicates that the origins of Rico's separation from his rebellious sexual organ lie in an ambivalent sexual episode with his mother. Rico, of course, ignores his friend's suggestions that he needs extended treatment; and to a large degree so do we. Certainly we distrust the narrator – our sympathies, and Moravia's, lie in the end with the penis and not its owner – but we readily translate Rico's unique and exaggerated experience into the common one. Only an undercurrent of strangeness remains as implied comment on the normal male's relationship to his sexual organ.

The works by Ferreri, Roth and Moravia have striking similarities in their conception. All of them are products of the 1970s, and it may be this decade's new ideas of maleness that they reflect. Of even more interest, however, than articulated ideas about the penis is the possibility of a common style encouraged by this particular subject matter. The penis as model for artistic style is acknowledged by Claes Oldenburg, who has asserted that he seeks 'an art that twists and extends and accumulates and spits and drips, and is heavy and coarse and blunt and sweet and stupid as life itself'.[10] Hence his giant lipsticks, his fleshy typewriters, his flaccid, drooping percussion sets. The visual reminiscences in such constructions simultaneously convey a strangeness in the penis and in the commonplace objects rendered in its style. Without such explicit visual reminiscences, however, it becomes much more difficult to identify any verbal style that is particularly appropriate to the penis. In literature, the closest thing to Oldenburg's preoccupations is James Joyce's denomination of two adjacent styles in the Nausicaa episode of *Ulysses* as 'tumescence' and 'detumescence'. This can only be taken, though, as a private joke, a convenient metaphor for an inflated style followed by a flat one. Similarly, we have Hemingway, in *Death in the Afternoon*, commenting on what he calls 'erectile writing':

> It is well known, or not known, whichever you prefer, that due to a certain congestion or other, trees for example look different to a man in that portentous state and a man who is not. All objects look different. They are slightly larger, more mysterious, and vaguely blurred. Try it yourself. Now there has or had arisen in America a school of writers who (this is old Dr. Hemingstein the great psychiatrist deducing) had, it would seem, by conserving these congestions, sought to make all objects mystic through the slight distortion of vision that unrelieved turgidity presents.[11]

William Gass, for one, seems to take this theory seriously when he suggests that women 'lack that blood congested genital drive which energizes every great style.'[12] There is no point, though, in lingering over styles which have the terminology of the penis imposed upon them. It is a better idea to consider the styles in which the penis itself is usually described, and then to ask if any common denominator can be found.

The styles applied to the penis naturally reflect its qualities – which, as I have already indicated, are multiple and contradictory. Essentially, though, two qualities of the penis divide the field between them: its profundity and its comicality. Profundity is attested to by aeons of phallic worship, from ancient India to D.H. Lawrence. Yet the slang terms for that part of the body invariably have a comic overtone. This tone is altogether appropriate to something which, as Molly Bloom observes, looks at one moment like a turkey neck and gizzards and at the next like a hatrack. An arch comicality is also the quality of yet another monologue of a man to his penis – Robert Graves's 'Down, Wanton, Down!'

> Down, wanton, down! Have you no shame
> That at the whisper of Love's name,
> Or Beauty's, presto! up you raise
> Your angry head and stand at gaze?
>
> Poor bombard-captain, sworn to reach
> The ravelin and effect a breach –
> Indifferent what you storm or why
> So be that in the breach you die!
>
> Love may be blind, but love at least
> Knows what is man and what mere beast:
> Or Beauty wayward, but requires
> More delicacy from her squires.
>
> Tell me, my witless, whose one boast
> Could be your staunchness at the post,
> When were you made a man of parts,
> To think fine and profess the arts?
>
> Will many-gifted Beauty come
> Bowing to your bald rule of thumb,
> Or Love swear loyalty to your crown?
> Be gone, have done! Down, wanton, down!

The situation is the familiar one of a man at odds with his sexual organ. The tone, however, preserves that indifference and detachment which Bergson, for one, has made a condition of the comic effect. The narrator stands back, as it were, and watches the conflict between the part and the man as a whole. The witty personification of the penis, the imagery and the punning, are all observed by the poet with an ironical judiciousness. This may be compared with the hyperbolical use of personification, imagery, and wit found in both *Portnoy's Complaint* and *The Two of Us*. In these works the hyperbolic style reflects the hysteria of their narrators, and is the attempt to *create* a separation between themselves and their wayward organ. The words pour out for purposes of accusation, confession, purgation – not this cool and controlled imitation of despair, this wit that presupposes separation. Consequently the comic effect is undermined and riddled through with a genuine despair, to produce what Portnoy calls 'the comedy that *hoits*.'

The style that will do fullest justice to this subject must be one that will show simultaneously both its faces. It must mix a tragic sense with the comic – not in some Polonius-like layering of the modes, but in a way that is as rich and yet inevitably simple as the penis itself. In fact, if we trace back the ideas of tragic and comic to their origins in Greek culture, we ultimately trace them to the phallus: the dumb and visible symbol from which both spring. Greek theatre evolved from Dionysiac festivals. In the processions moving to the place of sacrifice a giant phallus was borne before the representation of Dionysos. Smaller phalli were carried by others in the procession. At the procession's end, while the sacrifice was being prepared, songs were sung which related events in the god's life – and it was these songs which evolved into Greek tragedy. At the same time, though, as the official religious procession made its way through the town, a semi-official group of revellers, the *komos*, accompanied it. They too had songs to sing, in honour of the phallus, while flinging witticisms to the boisterous crowd. Their songs were called comedies. And these revellers likewise carried the phallus tied to their belt or hung from their neck. This element was carried over, and indeed stressed, as comedy evolved from its improvised beginnings. The actors in Old Comedy wore flesh-coloured jerkins with an exaggerated phallus of red leather attached. The phallus is thus the symbol which presides over the primitive origins of both tragedy and comedy; in the same context it evokes simultaneously veneration and mockery with no apparent sense of contradiction.

Lawrence has already suggested the style which expresses this primitive fusion with the fullest sense of its implications: it is the grotesque. Amid all the controversy over how to define such a rich and protean form as the grotesque, most writers on the subject have agreed with Ruskin that it is basically characterized by a combination of the ludicrous and the terrible. Other characteristics also indicate its appropriateness to the penis: the grotesque tends to exaggerate, to go to extremes; yet it is strongly linked with reality, especially physical reality; it tends to deform the sense of an ordered, controlled whole by a wilfulness of parts. At the beginning of his *Pantagruel*, for instance, Rabelais creates a gallery of grotesques by the simple device of swellings in the body caused by eating fruit. Some grow bellies huge as wine-vats, some grow ears as large as cloaks, and some grow members as long as soldiers' lances. Now of the various extraordinary swellings described, it is the last which is a part of the ordinary life of the male – scaled down, of course, from the giants of those days. In the penis one can still, within a few moments, sense the force of the grotesque in motion, sense the *process* of wilfully exaggerating a physical part at the expense of the whole. That is one reason why Mikhail Bakhtin, in his analysis of Rabelais, stresses

> those parts of the grotesque body in which it outgrows its own self, transgressing its own body, in which it conceives a new, second body: the bowels and the phallus. These two areas play the leading role in the grotesque image, and it is precisely for this reason that they are predominately subject to positive exaggeration, to hyperbolization; they can even detach themselves from the body and lead an independent life. . . .[13]

He observes in passing that the nose, that favourite subject of grotesque art, can also in a way detach itself from the body. But the nose symbolizes the phallus in Rabelais, as in his folkloric sources. Recent scholarship has emphasized this aspect of Gogol as well.

In art, the grotesque is plainly the style in which the penis, especially the erect penis, is rendered. Examples may be found in all the varied emphases and shadings of the grotesque: in the witty, elegant style of a Pompeian tripod; the irresistible Dionysiac force of a Picasso engraving; the bumptious obscenity of Beardsley's illustrations to *Lysistrata*. In literature, things are less plain. However, we may discern some salient features of the grotesque in the two major examples I have brought forward, by Roth and Moravia.

1 *The ludicrous and terrible combined*. Portnoy, as he himself observes, is inside a classic example of the Jewish joke. Without the detachment which is a condition of the comic effect, his situation is purely terrible to him. Certainly many of his actions – like what young Alex does to his family's liver dinner – are really rather awful; they are also outrageously funny. Though his 274-page monologue culminates in a scream, it is only to be followed by a 'punch line', which any sensitive reader would have to find both ludicrous and terrible: 'So [said the doctor]. Now vee may perhaps to begin. Yes?' In similar ways, Moravia's Rico is often funny to the reader, though not to himself; and our laughter has its initial impulse in shock.

2 *Exaggeration and excess*. It begins, in *The Two of Us*, with the table of contents: Desublimated! Expropriated! Mystified! Frustrated! – each one-word chapter title is followed by a melodramatic exclamation mark. What this indicates is a state of psychological excess that outdoes even the physical excesses which are supposed to evoke it. Portnoy's state of mind is similarly histrionic, almost hysterical. It is a state of mind reflected in the work's structure: sprawling, though energetic, with parts constantly shooting away from any ordered progression of the whole.

3 *The warping of the 'normal'*. 'The grotesque is the estranged world,' asserts Wolfgang Kayser.[14] The phallic existence of both Portnoy and Rico estranges them from the normal world, and both of them do in fact need the treatment of their psychiatrists. That normal men quite easily identify with both protagonists does not invalidate this judgment; it invites further speculation on the nature of normal men. Portnoy and Rico share an 'ambivalently abnormal' vision which has a certain wild energy. Especially in Portnoy, a reckless agility of mind and tongue rings in the most disparate – or desperate – associations. Rico, while

less mobile, often metamorphoses the object of his vision into a collection of oddly assorted images. An example is his view of Mafalda, his boss's wife. She is described in terms of a dinosaur with huge hind-quarters, and has a long neck like a serpent's, surmounted by the tiny face of 'an old cat or an elderly Pekinese dog'. The combination of heterogeneous images was one of the commonest techniques of the grotesque when it was still a style of decoration found in artificial grottoes. Here, however, it conveys the sensation of a certain psychological state.

4 *Lack of resolution*. Philip Thomson suggests as a definition of the grotesque 'the unresolved clash of incompatibles in work and response.'[15] This is far too general to stand as a definition, but it may certainly be accepted as an important characteristic. In both the novels we are considering, the incompatibles remain un-resolved, whether at the level of descriptive detail or overall structure. Each work concludes with only a final grotesque twist to emphasize that the protagonist has gotten nowhere. Port-noy's final cry – indeed his whole complaint – is utterly futile, as the punch line clearly indicates. And Rico ends by returning to his wife, penis swollen with its own triumph.

> Fausta's hand undid the chain, the door opened, and she appeared on the threshold in her dressing-gown. She looked at me, looked down, saw 'him' and then, without saying a word, put out her hand to take hold of 'him,' as one might take hold of a donkey's halter to make it move. Then she turned her back to me, pulling 'him' in behind her, and, with 'him,' me. She went into the flat, 'he' went behind her; I followed them both.

The man here submits to his penis, only to have the penis in its turn abjectly submit to a woman. In this way, Moravia closes his novel with the image of a double lack of control for the man. The erect penis, which should be the sign of male power, has become instead the sign of his helplessness. However, I do not want to give the impression that this is a degeneration peculiar to this century. In classical Greece the phallus was the very symbol of *arete*, the masculine ideal of virtue or nobility; it might also express a lack of control threatening to that idea. One vase of the fifth century BC shows a woman marching off with a giant disembodied phallus tucked under her arm: it could well serve as an illustration for Moravia's novel.[16] The penis has been viewed with ambivalence from the first, as we have seen, and it continues to be so viewed. It is that view, and not the physical appendage, which is being portrayed in the Greek era and in this one – in every era. The fig leaf has not really dropped, and never will.

The ways of portraying the penis today carry on many of the practices of preceding centuries. That part has been personified before, in the Roman god Fascinus for one. The qualities of independence and assertiveness so important to the twentieth-century version underlie many of the earlier metaphors, such as those of Cleland and De Sade. The difference is that now the independent, assertive penis trails behind it an individual human being. The sense of helpless alienation between the man and his sexual organ gives a more intense expression to what is now more a psychological than a physical vision. We are able to sense something that extends beyond the flesh-and-blood penis; and that thing is the uneasy relationship that a man may have to the root of his own manhood.

CHAPTER 5

The novel as a dirty joke

Robert Kroetsch is a Canadian novelist with an overly active muse. His practice is to write a novel once, and then to 'layer' it – to fold in more patterns of imagery, more ingenious catastrophes, more elliptical and eloquent phrasing. Occasionally, his books will accumulate so many layers that they begin to sag, their original vitality suffocated under a multitude of special effects. It is the literary vice of over-writing. But our vices and our virtues often come down to the same qualities, viewed in different ways; and so it is with Kroetsch. At his best, he produces novels whose elements are so intricately locked together that they become richly thought-provoking. Such are his *Badlands* and *The Studhorse Man*; and what these books provoke us to think about are masculinity, and writing, and the relationship between the two. Because Kroetsch is a consciously masculine writer, it is tempting to explain his lapses by Woolf's notion that it is fatal for writers to be conscious of their sex. However, Kroetsch is far from writing with only one side of his brain. If his writing strikes a macho stance, it also incorporates an opposition to that stance, and plays out the tension that results.

Badlands is a good example. It is the story of an expedition made in 1916 by a hunchback named William Dawe and a few male companions to find dinosaur skeletons. We are told about this expedition fifty-six years later by Dawe's daughter Anna, whose telling is part of her own attempt to reconstruct the past. William and Anna both write about the expedition: the difference between the *ways* that they write about it suggests something about differing male and female attitudes to words.

What William Dawe writes are 'field notes': Kroetsch has recently adopted this as the title of his collected poems. His intent in doing this is undoubtedly ironic; for William's field notes are terse, and obviously inadequate to the experience they claim to record. Anna describes them as 'cryptic notations made by men who held the words themselves in contempt but who needed them nevertheless in order to carry home, or back if not home, the only memories they would ever cherish: the recollections of their male courage and their male solitude.'[1] The male contempt for words is spat out in one of William's field notes:

> *I despise words*, he wrote; he stared at the sentence, enjoying it. Writing it down had freed him, in some way he did not fully comprehend. *Had a dream last night*, he wrote. Not intending to add what the dream had been, that in the night . . . he had dozed into a wakeful sleep; a fantasy had assaulted him while he lay helpless on his back on the deck of the flatboat. And he added: *You and a lover met at your cottage on Georgian Bay. He invited you in swimming. You saw a snake in the water and panicked and drowned*. Dawe thinking: I'm losing hold of myself, too much time in the sun today, running in the dark last night when I should have ordered the boat ashore. And he wrote, carefully, deliberately, to conclude the paragraph with a mere statement of fact and reason: *No sign of my bow-man or my maps*. (p. 34).

A well-rounded paragraph indeed. Every emotional connection or resonance has been excised, and the writing hops from one truncated sentence to another. We have the mere skeleton of what was once alive. The field notes are as fossilized as the expedition's goal.

Anna writes very differently. Where William 'wrote quickly, staving off the words that swarmed into his mind' (p. 37), Anna proliferates words, fleshing out emotion, tone and detail. Hers are the rich extrapolations of the born novelist. Yet she, like many women, suffers 'the anxiety of authorship' and feels that it is not her proper business to tell tales: 'Why it was left to me to mediate the story I don't know: women are not supposed to have stories. We are supposed to sit at home, Penelopes to their wars and their sex.' (p. 3). Anna's gift for full and sensitive narration is apparently the polar opposite of William's curt male annotations. Yet even as she weaves her story, a nagging doubt in her tends to unravel it. She fears falling into the ready-made novelistic patterns, which are male ways of controlling and subduing experience no less than are William Dawe's tight-lipped denials. Speaking for all women now, Anna distrusts

> . . . the curious little narrative tricks of a male adventure: the lies that enable the lovers to meet, the mystery of who did the killing, the suspense before victory. As if we didn't know all the answers long before they asked their absurd questions. . . . They have their open spaces, and translate them into a fabled hunting. We have only time to survive in, time, without either lies or mystery or suspense: we live and then die in time. (p. 27).

Of one of Dawe's crew, Anna writes: 'Total and absurd male that he was, he assumed, like a male author, an omniscience that was not ever his, a scheme that was not ever there.' (p. 76). As female author, Anna is more uneasy in her role; yet her distrust of words links her, in a curious way, to the total and absurd male that is her father.

Kroetsch's attitude to words in *Badlands* does not finally settle on either masculine or feminine modes of writing. The contrast between Anna's narration and William's only heightens our awareness of how peculiar an act it is to write at all. Something of that peculiarity is captured in a description which, on the face of it, appears to be merely about the act of towing a flatboat down a river.

> The burdened boat, Dawe motionless and writing in its center, seemed to move of its own: it floated square and lifeless on its own image while the three figures half immersed in the water themselves both fled the image and dragged it along behind them: they leaned against the line with fanatic determination, the line at times disappearing down into the water as if they'd hooked onto the uncreated world itself, would pull it out of the depths. (p. 240).

The passage, like the boat, carries the burden of the writing act. The 'line' is not just a rope here but any written line, for writing too emerges out of depths unknowable to us. Somehow a whole 'uncreated world' comes into being; the blank page, 'square and lifeless', is filled. In reading the page we enter that same amphibian existence: half on the surface of words, and half in depths we only dimly comprehend; at the risk of over-allegorizing, I would suggest a significance even to the impulse that simultaneously flees the image and drags it after. It is the basic human predicament in regard to words. No matter who is using them, words continually attempt to transcend themselves, to communicate something that is beyond words. So nobody ever has the last word: we flee our own images always, towards new ones. At the same time, we drag the images along behind us, because language often determines the way we will perceive and therefore what we perceive. Our new perceptions must then be put into words in the same ambiguous and never-ending process. All these powerful suggestions are connected – literally, in the description – to the simple image of William Dawe 'motionless and writing'.

While in *Badlands* the problem of writing is approached from both a masculine and feminine perspective, Kroetsch gives us an exclusively masculine version in *The Studhorse Man* – his best-known book. The Penelope figure here, a statuesque virgin named Martha Proudfoot, stays at home in a small Alberta town and writes nothing. Meanwhile her fiancé of thirteen years, Hazard Lepage, is embarked on an odyssey of philandering, while leading his big blue stallion from farm to farm to provide stud service. But he writes nothing either. The self-proclaimed author of 'this portentous volume' is Martha's virginal cousin, Demeter Proudfoot. The feminization which many males attach to writing may be reflected in Demeter's name, given to him erroneously by a mother not well versed in the classics. And since Kroetsch is fond of giving his characters loaded names (e.g. Roger Dorck, Miss Kundt) we may find some of the riskiness of writing reflected in the name of Hazard Lepage. The risk here may well be one peculiar to males – namely that they will suffer a diminution of their masculinity. Demeter, of course, has a different version of that risk:

> The biographer is a person afflicted with sanity. He is a man who must first of all be sound of mind, and in the clarity of his own vision he must ride out the dark night, ride on while all about him falls into chaos. The man of the cold eye and the steady hand, he faces for all of humanity the ravishments and the terrors of existence.[2]

This sounds good, if a trifle orotund. Knowing more about Demeter, however, causes us to call into question his whole version of the writer's risk. It becomes apparent that, far from being 'sound of mind', Demeter is a patient in an insane asylum. Like Marat, he writes from a bathtub:

> Sometimes of a morning I fold a three-by-five card into a little triangular hat and set it square on my perky fellow's noggin and pirates we sail here together in my bathtub, our cargo the leather-bound books and the yellowing scribblers, the crumbling newspaper clippings and the envelopes with their canceled stamps and the packs of note-cards that make up the booty of our daring. (p. 38)

Here he sees himself as pirate; earlier he has painted himself as a cross between the Lone Ranger and Dürer's Knight. He is the masculine hero: his penis is piratical sidekick, looting god knows what; or he rides the horse which is throughout the book a symbol of phallic potency. In actual fact, Demeter remains virginal, passive, and obviously prone to delude himself about the nature of his literary endeavours. Like many another male author, he would like to see writing as a species of manly action; he would like it to be a match for the rowdy actions of his biographical subject, Hazard. However, the correspondence does not hold. Instead, Demeter and Hazard illustrate one of Anna Dawe's musings: 'Action and voice: how strange they should have so little connection.'[3]

The contrast between Demeter and Hazard is underscored by the language each uses. Demeter's language is literary: complexly structured and polysyllabic, it seems on the whole effeminate. Contributing to this impression are Demeter's word choices, such as his use of 'forbidden' adjectives ('a lovely china pot'). Hazard, on the other hand, uses the language of men. This is not just because he is manly but also because he may be 'very nearly illiterate' – under the circumstances, a rather manly thing to be. Even though Demeter narrates this work, we have the occasional breakthrough of Hazard's own words. The contrast to Demeter's style is significant:

> . . . the scent of spring was in that yeasty wind, the high raw odor of mares and spring –

Already I find myself straying from the mere facts. I distort. I must control a certain penchant for gentleness and beauty. Hazard did not say 'mares and spring.' We were chatting together on the ranch where finally I caught up with him and he said in his crude way, 'That raw bitch of a wind was full of crocuses and snatch.' (p. 13)

Crude as Hazard may be, Demeter is by his own admission 'sometimes enthralled by his very crudeness'. (p. 11) This must be extended beyond language alone to apply as well to Hazard's brawling action and his sexual activity. It becomes more and more clear as the novel progresses that Demeter, who voices such strong moral disapproval of Hazard, is secretly attracted to him, wishing in a sense to *become* him. One way of taking over Hazard's life is to write it. Kroetsch himself has referred to 'the biographer in *The Studhorse Man* slowly usurping the subject of his biography'.[4] And the usurpation through writing is parallel to the usurpation which actually takes place in Hazard's life. In a sense, Demeter has always aspired to Hazard's position. He has cherished a long and hopeless passion for Martha, which may arise as much as anything else from a desire to supplant Hazard in the saddle, so to speak. His real feelings emerge with startling intensity when Hazard is brought home apparently dead, having been retrieved from a burning house where he had been engaged in some last-ditch dalliance with a certain Mrs Laporte. Rather than rejoice, even momentarily, that now he is free to make Martha his own, Demeter suffers a well-nigh total collapse, and undergoes a significant transformation. For instance: Demeter, who has been working in a beer parlour, says that at Hazard's death he 'had come to recognize the futility of all labor and would not thereafter labor again'. And he adds, 'Wisdom comes strangely to our reluctant minds.' (p. 146) Demeter's mind may still be reluctant to realize that his abnegation of labour makes him more like the irresponsible Hazard. However, Demeter is forced to realize – indeed, to make real – his desire to assume Hazard's role when it develops that Hazard is not dead, but only overcome by smoke. His body has been prematurely stored in the icehouse, in lieu of a morgue, where it is visited by Martha. At this point Hazard rises from the dead – and the first part of him that rises is his penis, under the tentative touch of the virginal Martha. Becoming increasingly less tentative, Martha brings him back to life: *she* then becomes the rider facing down the dark night.

With his union to Martha, Hazard has closed his odyssey. He will settle down; he will give up his long search for the perfect mare to mate with his great blue stallion in order to propagate the Lepage breed. And he will presumably give up his own matings. But Demeter will not give up. In terms that are almost the same as those of Martha's 'love and pity and concern' for 'Old Blue', as Hazard calls his penis, Demeter decides that his 'devotion and concern' will save the blue stallion from being the last of his breed. He steals the stallion along with Martha's five Arabian mares and takes them to Hazard's own house, which he turns into a kind of fort. This move is plainly not necessary to propagate the breed, if the breed in question is only an equine one: Martha would of her own accord grant Hazard access to her mares. It is the breed that Hazard himself represents that is threatened by the capitulation to domesticity, for he is a vanishing form of masculine life. That he has undergone a turnabout of his own is underscored by the circumstances of his death when, in attempting to sneak into the house, he is trampled by his own panicked stallion. It is left unclear whether he was really trying to retrieve the horse or to retrieve Martha, who has now become a half-willing hostage. We only know that Demeter refuses to shoot the stallion as it stands astride the stunned Hazard, though Martha begs him to:

'Kill him now. Hazard is still breathing.'
'He's all that Hazard lived for,' I said.
'No,' Martha said.

And then it is too late. The stallion crushes Hazard's head.

His death fulfils in a number of ways the prophecy of an old Frenchwoman to the young Hazard: *La mer sera votre meurtrière*. The blue stallion is called Poseidon; but also, in a punning way, the 'murderess' is the 'mare' – the woman for whom Hazard jeopardizes himself in the end. Finally, the blue stallion is emblematic of Hazard's 'Old Blue', the phallic impulse which draws him through his life and to his death. As is common with Kroetsch, we have an embarrassment of riches here. The last two interpretations are almost directly opposed, making male and female principles simultaneously responsible for Hazard's death. Both interpretations are supported elsewhere in the book. When Hazard is asked by a little old nun 'Why do you wish to find the mare?' he is confused by her slight accent and understands her to say 'la mer'. When the same nun offers him permanent asylum and a steady income, the sorely tempted Hazard harangues his horse – or the principle he represents: 'No! You four-legged cock! No!' Of course he does hit the road again, even though, as William New has pointed out, Hazard is dragged through life protesting 'No!' and 'Stop!' What he is protesting may well be the autocracy of the cock, however many legs it has. These two interpretations can in fact be resolved: to a man who lives in this intensely phallic mode, the woman may well imply death. No matter how strenuously the Don Juan pursues women in general, or one by one, the idea that one woman should be his mate represents a kind of death, for she will mean the end of his former life. Thus P. Cockburn, curator of the Provincial Museum, takes Hazard in and installs him in a large historical four-poster, surrounded by a wax museum of Canadian noteworthies. Compliant to her desires, Hazard 'screws the ass off her'. But he slips away before morning, leaving a waxen figure in his place. P. Cockburn has promised, or threatened, to make a waxen model of him; and 'he would not be seduced, he was resolved, into that immortality.' (p. 33) That immortality is of course equivalent to death, as mortuary science might see it; and also to a form of permanent possession. If to a man a woman may thus represent a kind of death, Kroetsch also represents death as if it were a woman: 'Death was a nightmare presence bent on snuffing Hazard into a longer darkness; it was the crone and succubus, the ancient fiend turned female that in the night of dream has fatal intercourse with men.' (p. 148) Curiously enough, this statement is made even while Martha is having intercourse with Hazard in order to bring him back to life. But male fears about women are not so easily dismissed, not even by realities.

Certainly *The Studhorse Man* is a death-centered book, as are most works by the School of Virility. It ends with the death of its most manly protagonist; and it opens *in medias mortis*, with Hazard trapped in an icy boxcar full of 'BONES FOR WAR' (theoretically, they will help to make fertilizer, like many of the soldiers then doing their duty as men). But I am probably giving the impression that this novel is tragic and terribly solemn, which is not the case. If death is prominent in it, humour is even more so. *The Studhorse Man* is quite simply a very funny book. The episode with P. Cockburn is an example. It is followed by a chase after Hazard in the style of the Keystone Cops. Hazard finds safety with the old nun in a Home for the Incurables populated by sex-obsessed geriatric cases, again to good comic effect. Kroetsch has said that he was once 'very much into the theory of comedy'.[5] *The Studhorse Man* demonstrates its practice on almost every page.

In order to understand this novel's odd mix of *machismo*, humour and death it is useful to get into the theory of comedy, like Kroetsch. The most useful branch of that wide-ranging theory is one which is often overlooked: the theory of the dirty joke. There is something comic about this phrase in itself; the dirty joke is hardly thought of as a literary form that would lend itself to theories. However, what few theories exist may find their application here. We have seen that macho literature often incorporates popular modes such as slang and obscenity. The dirty joke is akin to these; and its transmogrification may tell us much about writing in the masculine mode.

To begin with, there are in Kroetsch's book actual sessions in which everyone joins in telling dirty jokes. One of these, predictably, is at a wedding:

> I found Hazard . . . with a group of men around the beer kegs. They were all of them cracking lewd jokes, now and then breaking into a jig, each man alone. . . .
> 'What's the fastest two-handed game in the world?' somebody wanted to know. (p. 101)

Another session, less predictably, arises out of a funeral:

> 'This undertaker,' a farmer from St. Leo was saying, 'he was preparing a body when he noticed the fellow had the biggest whang he had ever laid eyes on. He called in a friend who was just then doing a little work in the next room. "Look at this," he says to his friend. "Did you ever see one like this?" "I've got one just like it," the friend says. "The hell you have. That big?" the undertaker says. "No," the friend says, "That dead." '

> The laughter was enormous. . . . 'I'll bet Mrs Laporte could
> have raised it,' someone added, and got a few more lascivious
> laughs. (p. 144)

We have been listening to the reaction of beer parlour patrons at
the news of Hazard's presumed death. It is significant that the
content of these jokes forms the basis for the novel's next scene –
only it is not Mrs Laporte but Martha who raises Hazard from the
dead. This clear example of the relationship between the novel
and the dirty joke encourages us to look for other ways in which
the characteristics of this kind of humour may underlie
Kroetsch's book. Its picaresque mode, for instance, though a
venerable literary tradition, may in this case be related to the
usual mode of telling dirty jokes. There is no real continuity in
such a joke-telling session. One joke is no sooner told than it is
followed by another, usually under the pretence of 'topping'
its predecessors. In his improbable and monumental opus
Rationale of the Dirty Joke, Gershon Legman compares joke-telling
to Don Juanism. As in a series of one-night stands, each joke is
told once and once only; a session of dirty jokes rouses an appe-
tite that is never sated, but must always move on to something
new.[6] The attitude is like Hazard's own in regard to women.

We can find out more about Hazard's attitudes by considering
the particular dirty jokes he tells or lives out. For the jokes that a
person habitually tells are often really about the teller, revealing
deep-seated fears and hidden desires. So the laughter that
follows will function as a shriving after the joke's 'confession',
Legman claims. To him, it is axiomatic that 'a person's favorite
joke is the key to that person's character.'[7] In making these
claims, Legman is only following Freud. For Freud, 'laughter
arises when the sum total of psychic energy, formerly used for
the occupation of certain psychic demands, has become unuti-
lizable so that it can experience absolute discharge.' Thus the
heartiest and most genuine laughter is usually released in connection with areas such as sex, about which a listener is likely to
be most inhibited: '. . . as soon as he hears the joke, there
awakens within him compulsively and automatically a readiness
for this inhibition. This readiness for the inhibition . . . is simultaneously recognized as superfluous or as belated, and is thus
immediately discharged in its nascent state through the channel
of laughter.'[8]

If *The Studhorse Man*, then, is made up of dirty jokes, what is it that is being discharged? Not surprisingly, we find that the recurrent obsession here is phallic. This is clearly so in the undertaker joke and its subsequent acting out by Hazard and Martha. Hazard's very life depends upon his penis: if it can be resurrected, so can he. And as it expands, so does the rhetoric by which it is described:

> Martha was all curiosity to understand, to feel; and the mystery took form in her hand, became unshriveled and yet more the mystery, at once silk smooth and iron hard, boneless becoming bone of blood. There was no tree of knowledge to equal that one in her will to know, no ladder and no hill. *Axis mundi*, the wise men tell us, and on it the world turns. (p. 148)

An inflated claim – but certainly Hazard's world revolves around his prick. A humorous *flyting* between Hazard and a truck driver has earlier had them exchanging a whole array of phallic insults, beginning with the conventional 'peckerhead':

> 'You tool,' Hazard said. 'You faltering apparatus.'
> 'You whang and rod and pud,' the trucker replied. . . .
> Hazard saw his chance to drive away but missed it in order to shout, 'You dong.' He felt he was coming off rather badly in the exchange. 'You drippy dong. You johnny and jock.'
> The trucker in his excitement was beginning to stutter. 'You diddly dink. You d– you d– you d– you dink. You dick.'

During this exchange, we are told that 'the trucker was offending the very core of Hazard's being.' (p. 42) That core is obviously his penis. And since every penis exists as a series of deaths and resurrections, we have an insight into the curious rhythms of Hazard's life, with its picaresque alternations of catastrophic mock-deaths and comic triumphs. Rather than his penis being an extension of him, Hazard's life is an extension of his penis: 'A preposterous fate, to be at the mercy of something so rash, so reckless and fickle, so willful, unpredictable, stubborn – and so without morality.' (p. 59) This statement, entirely appropriate to Hazard's situation, is actually not about his relation to his own penis, but to his horse's, by which he makes his living. By now, though, it is clear that Hazard's 'Old Blue' and his big blue stallion correspond to each other: the stud is the man as much as the horse. Hazard's desire to extend the breed may be nothing more than an excuse to extend his own phallic mode of life.

However, the teller of this series of dirty jokes is not Hazard, nor even Demeter, but Robert Kroetsch. Any significance in the kind of jokes told should be applied to him. I should quickly add that I am not interested in making points about Kroetsch's putative sexual hang-ups. The phallic fixation here may be approached on quite another level; it tells us something about Kroetsch's attitudes to writing, conceived of as a masculine act. At this level, the phallus functions as a metaphor. Our concern is with (to cheerfully abuse a Lacanian term) the phallus as signifier. What its prevalence in *The Studhorse Man* signifies is a preoccupation with the act of signification itself. The fears of a lack of potency, the urge towards repeated resurrection, towards prolonging the breed – all these may be applied to the writer's relationship with his craft. Mailer comes close to recognizing this when he refers to his writer's ego as a 'ghost phallus'. Writing may then be conceived of as a sexual act, holding both risks and rewards for the male. Again and again, he hazards the page; firm, undaunted, he makes the muse moan.

Kroetsch himself seems to make this kind of identification. Asked point-blank about the connection between writing and the sex urge, he answered 'They're both acts of creation. And . . . both fail as well as succeed, are unpredictable. . . . In *The Studhorse Man*, the kind of trickster figure running through it, this irrational amoral impulse at work, is comparable to the writer.'[9] Kroetsch had read Paul Radin's work on the trickster figure in mythology just before writing *The Studhorse Man*; and the trickster has remained for him a favourite simile for all sorts of things. 'Language itself, the trickster, perhaps,' he writes in his journal.[10] Elsewhere he has said that in *The Studhorse Man* the trickster figure is the penis: 'they're both irrational, unpredictable. They do their own things.'[11] With no sense of strain, the same simile is applied to both the pen and the penis. They are seen to have the same characteristics, exactly those of Hazard's 'preposterous fate' in being dependent on a horse's cock for his livelihood.

Having established that Kroetsch connects his writing and his sexuality in these ways, I have to admit that this is not the whole picture. The tricks of the pen and the tricks of the penis have obvious differences as well as similarities; and a writer like Kroetsch will see them, at home in contradictions as he is. While there is a significant metaphorical parallel here, there is at the same time an opposition; and Kroetsch frequently makes use of it. In many of his novels there is a protagonist, who is active largely in sexual ways, and a passive narrator, whose version of action is to usurp the experience of the protagonist by writing about it. In *The Studhorse Man*, as we have seen, these roles are enacted by Hazard and Demeter. It is significant that Demeter describes himself in terms that recall the Lady of Shalott: 'By a fortunate combination of light and reflection, I am able to see out of my window without leaving my bathtub.' (p. 83) From this 'high window' Demeter can see, among other things, a road – a road along which Hazard once passed. The real world is outside his artistic solipsism: 'I myself prefer an ordered world, even if I must order it through a posture of madness.' (p. 59) Demeter is in this way a prisoner of his own artifice; and he attempts to imprison Hazard in that same artifice. This is a betrayal like that committed by one of Hazard's women: he discovers her coaxing his stallion towards an artificial vagina, to obtain the sperm necessary for artificial insemination. Hazard's horror at this seems disproportionate: if he is interested in extending the breed, this is a more efficient way of doing it than the complex negotiations often needed to get his stallion to mount a mare. His reaction becomes more comprehensible when we remember that the stallion represents his 'natural' phallic self; and all artifice is the opposition and the enemy of that self. In the end artifice wins. After Hazard's death, a use is found for his stallion: Poseidon impregnates mares at a rate beyond Hazard's wildest dreams – but only because the urine of pregnant mares is a source of oestrogen, which is used in the manufacture of birth control pills. The artifice that is 'this portentous volume' is no more to be trusted. This is not only because Demeter is a typically modern untrustworthy narrator. Literary artifice in itself may be viewed as the opposite pole, so to speak, from real phallic activity; it then threatens to replace the penis with the pen.

It is natural to ask where we may find Kroetsch in his own novel. Is he Demeter or Hazard, the writer or the roisterer? The answer, of course, is that he is neither and both. They are opposing selves within himself. In his journal Kroetsch has written about a similar opposition:

> We weave and unweave ourselves. The good person, gentle,
> kind, wise, considerate, a father and husband, a man who
> needs a wife, children, home. And then the son of a bitch who
> can't stand these things, the stud, the charlatan, the bastard,
> the wild drinking man, the deceiver and liar, the tell-tale
> self. . . . I don't know. But I do know something about Yeats
> and his opposing selves, and I do know that the risk of
> creation involves the risk of destruction.[12]

Creation and destruction may be seen in both opposing selves
here. Demeter creates the book and in doing so threatens to
destroy the reality of Hazard's existence by replacing it. Hazard
is creative in his own sexuality as well as in his aim to establish a
new breed of horse; but this sexual creativity is also destructive,
even self-destructive, in the ways we have seen. 'I think the
processes of creation and destruction operate simultaneously,'
Kroetsch has said. And he adds, 'That again is part of the comic
vision, a recognition of the totality of that relationship.'[13]

This brings us back to the comic vision, and back to the dirty
joke. The original question was about what was being discharged
in the dirty jokes of *The Studhorse Man*; and the answer is not one
that would have been apparent at the beginning. Underlying the
humour of the novel is a whole complex revolving around male
sexuality and writing. The two are held in a tense counterpoise
that involves as much mutual reinforcement as opposition. The
result is bound to be an intense ambivalence and, resulting from
this, anxiety. The psychological situation is made to order for a
joke. Release comes in a gust of laughter without the need for
overly psychoanalytical probing – in accordance with Mailer's
warning against 'digging too close to the source of one's work'. If
this novel is Kroetsch's confession, he is shriven and forgiven
through our laughter. Even the prevalence of death in the book,
especially at the end, does not tip the balance. Indeed the
humorous context may be what makes it possible to incorporate
these death-fears, whether actual or merely phallic.

The Studhorse Man as a whole is finely balanced between creation and destruction. Like Demeter, like Hazard, Kroetsch does
both simultaneously. In one sense, this novel's creation destroys,
by usurping them, any number of other novels that might have

been written from the same starting-point. In another sense, the impulse to begin an act of creation at all is an impulse to purge – that is, destroy – a complicated cluster of emotions. You write to get it out of your system. And you tell dirty jokes for exactly the same reason. The joke is created as an artistic form (admittedly a degraded one); Freud explains how this form instinctively mimics the natural processes of the unconscious. Psychic energy surrounding an area of tension is thereby released and immediately realized to be unnecessary. This release and this realization provokes that sudden outburst of delight we call laughter. Something has been created – the joke – in order that something else may be destroyed – our tensions and anxieties. In Kroetsch's case, these tensions and anxieties have to do with the act of literary creation and his relation to it as a male who is at least partly stud, son of a bitch, bastard and so forth. Any hyper-male has a store of anxieties locked up by powerful inhibitions. If he is a writer, ambivalent attitudes to writing may contribute to that store; but his writing can provide release. If he is a more usual kind of man, he will accomplish the same thing by telling dirty jokes. One activity is seen as infinitely more worthwhile than the other. Yet the same impulses may account for the existence of the highly wrought novel and the casual joke.

CHAPTER 6

A fabled hunting

When Mailer, in *The Prisoner of Sex*, writes that 'a man can hardly ever assume he has become a man' he is expressing a predicament typical of his time. Men today can at best 'assume' that they are men – hoping that their assumptions are not self-deluding – instead of officially assuming their manhood at a specific time and place. The rite of passage is dead. It has dwindled into a Bar Mitzvah, where the boy need do nothing to earn his manhood but survive until thirteen; or it has become a purely private passage – the surreptitious loss of one's virginity. Neither of these is likely to convince a boy that he is fundamentally changed, both in his own eyes and in those of others. But the power of a rite of passage still glimmers through an activity primitive in itself, and undertaken in a spirit of masculine community: I am speaking of the hunt. William Faulkner's story 'The Old People' is an example. The boy Quentin is brought up with guns, and shoots his share of squirrels and rabbits. Not until he is nine, though, is he allowed to come with the men to their annual hunting camp; and then he can only take the stand that is assigned him, and wait for the buck deer whose blood will initiate him into manhood. He complains to Sam Fathers, his mentor and teacher:

> 'I'll never get a shot,' I said. 'I'll never kill one.'
> 'Yes you will,' Sam said. 'You wait. You'll be a hunter. You'll be a man.'

Sam's prediction is fulfilled when the boy is twelve: he shoots his buck and 'ceased to be a child and became a hunter and a man.' Sam then dips his hands in the blood of the freshly-slain deer and wipes them back and forth over the boy's face. This marks him: he has been baptized in blood. A less ritualized initiation, but an initiation nevertheless, is described by Hemingway in 'The Short Happy Life of Francis Macomber'. Here it is a full-grown man who finally comes into his manhood. He achieves it the hard way, while on safari, by first losing everything when he flees a charging lion. In the next day's hunting, however, he rallies and, by some logic of the psyche, breaks through to the discovery of his own courage. It is like the entry into a new life – a life that is destined to be short indeed. That same day, while standing up to the charge of a wounded water buffalo, Macomber is shot by his castrating wife, perhaps accidentally. Both these stories, though they depict the moment of initiation, are really about other subjects: in Faulkner's case, the continuity of blood; and in Hemingway's, the relations between men and women. However, manhood itself is the theme of three novels which deal with the hunt as initiation: James Dickey's *Deliverance*, Mailer's *Why Are We in Vietnam?* and Robert F. Jones's *Blood Sport*.[1] All three of these develop their theme in such detail that we are not just presented with the moment of initiation, but with an extended anatomy of what it is we are being initiated into.

Such an instructive component is in fact part of the initiation process as anthropology outlines it. Male puberty rites generally fall into four parts. First, the boy is removed from society and taken into the wilderness. Second, he receives instruction on the lore and myths of the tribe. Third, he passes through an ordeal: he may undergo a simulated death; or endure pain, as in circumcision; or hunt and kill a dangerous animal. Fourth, the initiate returns to society and is welcomed as a man. The purpose of such an initiation is plainly not just to commemorate change but to produce it. So these novels, each of which is based on this four-part structure, are studies of how change occurs.

Upon first going into the wilderness, Ed Gentry, the narrator of *Deliverance*, confronts himself in a new role:

> . . . I caught a glimpse of myself in the rear mirror. I was light green, a tall forest man, an explorer, guerilla, hunter. I liked the idea and the image, I must say. Even if this was just a game, a charade, I had let myself in for it; and I was here in the woods, where such people as I had got myself up as were supposed to be. Something or other was being made good. I

touched the knife hilt at my side, and remembered that all men were once boys, and that boys are always looking for ways to become men. (p. 69)

At this point, of course, he is only playing the role. However, that is the first step in becoming the role, in assuming it as one's own. Though it is only an image or costume that Ed admires, yet superficial trappings have the power to create certain expectations, not only in onlookers but also in one's self. When Ed leaves his home in a car burdened with the tools of the woodsman, he thinks to himself that he will have to live up to his equipment. Actions which are at first dictated by externals, then, come to have an internal conviction. Ed wakes early on the first morning after making camp, and takes his bow and arrows off into the foggy woods. At first, this is only a performance for the benefit of the others; but soon 'hunting and pretending to hunt had come together and I could not now tell them apart'. (p. 95) Eventually he goes through a deadlier version of hunting: Ed climbs to the top of a cliff from which he expects a murderer will try to pick off his companions at dawn. Yet, he tells us, 'I still had no real belief that the man would come; it was far more likely that I had figured the whole thing wrong. I was just going through motions, even though they were the motions of life and death.' (p. 186) The mere motions lead smoothly and inevitably to going through with the real thing.

Going through the motions, again, is how Ed learns to paddle, the first time he gets into a canoe: 'movies and pictures of Indians on calendars gave me a general idea of what to do, and I waved the paddle slowly through the water, down and along the left side of the canoe.' (p. 73) The movies provide his moves here; and throughout the book, movies seem to represent all those improbable models by which a man structures his experiences. When Ed and his friends have been spilled out of their canoes into the river, the movies incongruously come to mind.

From where we were the cliff looked something like a gigantic drive-in movie screen waiting for an epic film to begin. I listened for interim music, glancing now and again up the pale curved stone for Victor Mature's stupendous image, wondering where it would appear, or if the whole thing were not already playing, and I hadn't yet managed to put it together. (p. 147)

Ed's comment a while later is 'When do the movies start, Lord?' Only now the comment is provoked by hearing his own voice deliver lines he had not imagined himself capable of saying, lines about killing and being killed. Climbing up the cliff he searches for a handhold, 'remembering scenes in movies where a close-up of a hand reaches desperately for something, through a prison grate for a key, or from quicksand towards someone or something on solid ground.' (p. 164) During an attempt to imagine what he must do when he gets to the top of the cliff, Ed says, 'I could get there, in my mind. The whole thing focused, like an old movie that just barely held its own on the screen.' (p. 173)

The idea of focusing is also a way to conceive of the process of change.[2] Ed's first hunting expedition is a kind of dress rehearsal for his second, and it is characterized by its vague, unfocused quality. The fog through which he moves is an equivalent of his own state of mind; so that at the crucial moment his arrow misses the deer. As he makes plans for the more serious manhunt Ed thinks:

> In a way, it seemed already settled. It was settled as things in daydreams always are, but it could be settled only because the reality was remote. It was the same state of mind I had had when I had hunted the deer in the fog. These were worthy motions I was going through, but only motions . . . (p. 175)

This time, though, the motions are carried through in a moment whose quality of focus is made visually explicit. Ed sights down a tunnel he has cleared in a pine tree, and this frame encloses another frame, the peep sight of his bowstring. He kills his quarry essentially because the two of them have already come into a kind of common focus:

> For me to kill him under these conditions, he would have to be thinking as I had thought for him, and not approximately but exactly. The minds would have to merge. (p. 185)

And this is what has happened: 'I had thought so long and hard about him that to this day I still believe I felt, in the moonlight, our minds fuse.' (p. 180)

At the moment of fusion, Ed has attained a new focus, one that has shifted from the stagnant reality of his workday world to the world of the hunt. What is involved with the hunt, as Ortega y

Gasset views it, is 'a supremely free renunciation by man of the supremacy of his humanity'.[3] This supremacy is addressed in one of the epigraphs of *Deliverance*, from the book of Obadiah: 'The pride of thine heart hath deceived thee, thou that dwelleth in the clefts of the rock, whose habitation is high; that saith in his heart, who shall bring me down to the ground?' The other epigraph, from Georges Bataille, is more closely related to the first than one might think: 'Il existe à la base de la vie humaine, un principe d'insuffisance.' For his supremacy weighs heavily upon a man; he longs to shed the burden of civilization. Ed is convinced to go on the expedition simply by being asked what he plans on doing for the remainder of the day. Forced in this way to take a look at the quality of his normal existence, he returns to work at his ad agency feeling 'an enormous weight of lassitude' at 'the inconsequence of whatever I would do'. (p. 18) In view of the book's intensely masculine slant, it is significant that this vision of insufficiency is heralded by Ed's awareness, on his way to the office, that he is completely surrounded by women.

The shift made by Ed may be illustrated by one image, which itself shifts. On the morning of departure for the hunt, Ed wakes to the sound of a set of wind-chimes in the shape of an owl surrounded by birds. On the evening of the same day, Ed lies in his tent drifting off to sleep when a real owl lands on his tent. Its talons puncture the canvas in a way that echoes the waking fantasy in which Ed has been engaged. He replays in his mind the previous day's photography of an advertisement for ladies' underwear; only the kitten that has peeped over the model's shoulder is now made to put its claws in the panties in order to pull them down provocatively. In Ed's mind the scene explodes: 'She screamed, the room erupted with panic, she slung the cat round and round, a little orange concretion of pure horror, still hanging by one paw from the girl's panties, pulling them down, clawing and spitting in the middle of the air, raking the girl's buttocks and her leg-backs.' (p. 87) In both Ed's fantasy and the immediately following reality a claw has punctured a fabric shell, civilization's protective covering; and a whole alien mode of being intrudes, bestial and even terrifying. That alien mode of being is what the hunt is all about. The owl is a hunter: it uses the tent as a base between forays. Ed too will become a hunter: he will have the opportunity to fit into that fantasy and make it reality, just as the real owl has replaced the artificial one. Seeing the owl's talon in the canvas above his head, Ed reaches up and touches it. By so doing he signifies his acceptance of that breakthrough, the break away from civilization.

Ed attains a mode of being which has seemed alien to him. Yet it is made clear that this mode of being has always been within him, waiting to emerge. Thus, when Ed is spilled from his canoe, 'I got on my back and poured with the river, sliding over the stones like a creature I had always contained but never released.' (p. 144) What releases the new mode of being is often, as we have seen, a matter of externals – such things as dress, environment, stereotyped physical moves. Even having the face to suit the role is important. The night the men realize that Ed must climb the cliff towards a final reckoning he comments, 'It was a good thing we couldn't see faces. Mine felt calm and narrow-eyed, but it might not have been. There was something to act out.' (p. 151) Later, halfway up the cliff, Ed experiences a moment of pure vision at the centre of which is his own face, 'jaw set' in orthodox manly fashion. Plainly, whatever had to be acted out has now come out completely through Ed's actions. Acting out is role-playing which at some point turns into the real action demanded by the role. Something from within is allowed to emerge. And so, at the end of all the posturing, a man finds his authentic self.

That self, it could of course be argued, is no more authentic than is any mask that finally absorbs the face. But for most men, it *feels* authentic: something is 'being made good,' in Dickey's vague phrase. And what is being made good is an archetypal sense of what it means to be a man. There is a recurrent masculine nostalgia for an idea of the male that is simpler, more physical, and larger than life.[4] If this is an archetype, we can go further and say that the whole process of initiation into this idea of manhood also has a mythic resonance. When Ed first launches his canoe,

> a slow force took hold of us; the bank began to go backward. I felt the complicated urgency of the current, like a thing made of many threads being pulled, and with this came the feeling I always had at the moment of losing consciousness at night, going towards something unknown that I could not avoid, but from which I would return. (p. 73)

A passage like this encourages Frederic Jameson to argue that *Deliverance* can be seen as

> a journey into the unconscious itself, back to primal origins: a descent into the underworld, from which, after a battle with ogres or giants, limping painfully, one man lost and two others disabled, the heroes are at at length able to make their way back up into the light of day, bearing with them a story which can never be told. In the process, the most essential function of myth has been fulfilled: the creation of the hero.[5]

Jameson's phrasing echoes Joseph Campbell's description of the so-called 'monomyth':

> A hero ventures forth from the world of common day into a region of supernatural wonder: fabulous forces are there encountered and a decisive victory is won: the hero comes back from this mysterious adventure with the power to bestow boons on his fellow men.[6]

In turn, Campbell has seen in the monomyth a distinct parallel to the initiation ritual. When an initiation creates a man, it models him on a hero.

In the hunt-transformation of this masculine myth the supernatural forces encountered are not ogres or giants but animals. One has to think of animals as they are portrayed in primitive cave paintings, themselves executed as aids to the hunt. Animals possess a *mana* – a spiritual power – which may be the object of religious dread. When the hunter kills, he makes the animal's *mana* his own. This is always so, no matter to what degree the hunter does or does not understand it. We see a full and reverent understanding in Faulkner's 'The Old People'; we see – at least to begin with – a much more crassly materialistic version in Mailer's *Why Are We in Vietnam*?

In the Mailer novel, Rusty Jethroe's executive vanity demands that he brings back a grizzly from his Alaskan hunting trip; and this obsessiveness is accelerated into something like desperation after an embarrassingly botched attempt in the style of Francis Macomber ('Rusty was sick. He had to get it up. They had to go for grizzer now.'). Meanwhile his son's friend Tex has shot a wolf, and the guide enacts a ceremony like that of Sam Fathers:

Well, he got down and gave us each a cup of blood to drink
and that was a taste of fish, odd enough, and salt, near to
oyster sauce and then the taste of wild meat like an eye looking
at you in the center of a midnight fire, and D.J. was on with the
blood . . . D.J. next thing was on his hands and knees, looking
into that upper Yukon wolf mouth, those big teeth curved like
a tusk, and put his nose up close to that mouth, and thought
he was looking up the belly of a whale, D.J. was breathing wolf
breath, all the fatigue of the wolf running broken ass to the
woods and the life running the other way from him, a crazy
breath, wild ass odor, something rotten from the bottom of the
barrel like the stink of that which is unloved, whelp shit smell,
wild as wild garlic, bad, but going all the way right back into
the guts of things, you could smell the anger in that wolf's
heart (fucked again! I'll kill them!) burnt electric wire kind of
anger like he'd lived to rip one piece of flesh from another
piece, and was going to miss it now, going to miss going deep
into that feeling of *release* when the flesh pulls loose from the
flesh, and there D.J. was sweating, cause he was ready to get
down and wrestle with the wolf, and get his teeth to its throat,
his teeth had a glinty little little ache where they could think to
feel the cord of the jugular, it was all that blood he'd drunk, it
was a black shit fuel, D.J. was up tight with the essential
animal insanity of things. (pp. 69–70)

Mailer's familiar use of smell here conveys the animal's psychic
essence; and plainly something of that essence is transferred to
D.J. It is this kind of rapport with the animal which finally causes
D.J. and Tex to abandon the hunting party altogether, fed up
with its helicopter-aided, technologically streamlined slaughter.
They strike out on their own into the Alaskan mountains, leaving
behind almost all their equipment in what they call a 'purifica-
tion ceremony'. Their action is reminiscent of Quentin's in
another Faulkner story, 'The Bear', where the legendary animal
allows himself to be seen only when the young hunter divests
himself of everything, even his sense of direction. What the boys
eventually see, at least in their mind's eye, is a magnified version
of the wolf's spirit. As they lie outdoors under the flicker of the
Aurora Borealis,

    . . . the lights were talking to them, and they were going with it, near to, the lights were saying that there was something up here, and it was really here, yeah God was here, and He was real and no man was He, but a beast, some beast of a giant jaw and cavernous mouth with a full cave's breath and fangs, and secret call: come to me. They could almost have got up and walked across the pond and into the north without their boots, going up to disappear and die and join that great beast. In the field of all such desire D.J. raised his hand to put it square on Tex's cock and squeeze . . . (p. 202)

This is a sudden shift indeed from the mystical revelation of animal *mana* – thought not as unconnected as it may seem. Given the depth of this shared revelation, given what the two boys have gone through together, given their aloneness in this beautiful immensity, you would expect an intimacy, a love that finds expression in the sexual. You would be wrong. Yes, Tex and D.J. are 'crazy about each other', we are told, but 'fear not gentle auditer, they is men, real Texas men, they don't ding ding ring a ling on no queer street with each other' (p. 179), and there is no reason to imagine that they are having second thoughts now. What they are thinking of, as always, is upping the ante of their own manhood. All along, they have competed intensely; this is only another form of that competition. When Tex shoots the wolf, D.J. is 'half-sick having watched what Tex had done, like his own girl had been fucked in front of him and better, since he had had private plans to show Tex what real shooting might be. . . .' (p. 69) The indirect competition by means of trophy-taking, whether animal or sexual, or now cast aside for a more direct form: the trophy each wants is the other. It is each other's masculine *mana* that they covet now, and each thinks he can get it by turning the other into his 'woman' and possessing him. This is not love but rape:

D.J. . . . knew he could make a try to prong Tex tonight, there was a chance to get in and steal the iron from Texas' ass and put it in his own and he was hard as a hammer at the thought and ready to give off sparks and Tex was ready to fight him to death, yeah, now it was there, murder between them under all friendship, for God was a beast, not a man, and God said, 'Go out and kill – fulfill my will, go and kill' . . . (p. 203)

And they heed this commandment. The Dallas banquet at which D.J. claims to be remembering all this is a farewell to Tex and D.J., who on the next day will leave for Vietnam.

This last twist is really an inevitable transformation. Killing a man is only another way of acquiring his manliness. The hunters are no longer satisfied to take into themselves the *mana* of even the most dangerous animals. They seek now 'The Most Dangerous Game', as the title of Richard Connell's well-known story calls it; and that is man. To kill one's man is of course another primitive form of initiation into manhood. Ed Gentry's initiation explicitly takes this form; and when D.J., in his opening words, confesses that he 'has done animal murder, out out damn fart, and murder of the soldierest sort,' he is only referring to the same thing in two different ways.

For the initiate to kill is for him to learn something as well of what it is to be killed. The third stage of primitive rites mimics the boy's own death, or places him in actual danger of death, or teaches him at least about the nature of the body's pain. Ed's initiation is then more complete than D.J.'s – not just because he kills his man, but because he understands fully what that means. Ed kills a man he has 'fused' with; we may ask with Sophocles 'Who is the slayer, who the victim?' During the whole process he is forced into awareness of his actions and mental reactions; while D.J. is unlikely, we feel, to agonize much over what he is doing in Vietnam. Above all, what killing is about is the nature of the body – of being in the body, and of suffering bodily pain. *Deliverance* does full justice to this difficult form of knowledge.

For Dickey, 'the body is nothing less or more than the sense of being of a particular creature at a particular time and place. Everything he perceives and thinks depends upon his bodily state.'[7] Ed Gentry has this sense of his own being as body; an example is his expression of the curious incarnation involved in waking: 'I came up from the sleep-dark to the real dark of the room . . . and I lay with the room becoming actual around me, in the dark, beside my wife, in a body.' (p. 26) This kind of awareness is preparation for a more explicit philosophy which is articulated by Ed's mentor, Lewis. Himself the possessor of a magnificent build, Lewis sees the body in terms of survival. 'The body is the one thing you can't fake,' he says. 'It's just got to be there.' (p. 42) And he foresees a time when civilization will collapse and the body will be the only thing that *is* there. Lewis would seem to be proven right: the strength to hold a bow at full draw for a long time is needed for both Lewis and Ed to kill their man, thus ensuring survival. At the moment when Ed sees clearly what he must do, and do alone, Lewis rubs it in:

> 'Well,' he said, lying back, 'here we are, at the heart of the Lewis Medlock country.'
> 'Pure survival,' I said.
> 'This is what it comes to,' he said. 'I told you.' (p. 160)

Yet the body can provide something more than just survival. It can provide deliverance, which is a very different kind of thing. The two terms are subtly juxtaposed early in the book when Ed, while making love with his wife, imagines the gold-flecked eye of the model who had posed for the ad.

> . . . in the center of Martha's heaving and expertly working back, the gold eye shone, not with the practicality of sex, so necessary to its survival, but the promise of it that promised other things, another life, deliverance. (p. 28)

If deliverance is a matter of 'another life', then a sign of its advent occurs immediately after Ed's dialogue with Lewis. For, we are told, 'everything around me changed.' What has changed is actually Ed, as he finds himself newly born into a world of pure physical danger. His whole way of seeing is altered by this:

> . . . it was not seeing, really. For once it was not just seeing. It was beholding. I *beheld* the river in its icy pit of brightness, in its far-below sound and indifference, in its large coil and tiny points and flashes of the moon, in its long sinuous form, in its uncomprehending consequence. (p. 171)

Ed has come a long way from the state in which he left the city: 'My eyes kept hazing open and shut without seeing anything; things were in them but didn't have the power to stay or be remembered. The world was a kind of colored no-dream with objects in it.' (p. 39) This is the world from which Ed seeks to be delivered. It is not enough merely to change environments if he brings along the same old bodily state, upon which 'everything he perceives and thinks depends.'

At first Ed does not realize this. Feeling his complete severance

from daily routine on his first morning in the woods, Ed wonders
'Is this freedom?' A full answer only comes much later, after Ed
has killed his man. In the process he has gored himself with one
of his own arrows and now has to cut the arrow out of his side.
When he succeeds, he feels that 'there had never been a freedom
like it. The pain itself was freedom, and the blood.' (p. 195)
Freedom, then, lies not in the mere absence of routine; it lies in
the heart of the inhuman, the bestial: and it partakes of 'an
enormous physical indifference', like that of the man who has
scraped a knife over Ed's chest. Stripped of the civilized armour
which has both defended and imprisoned it, the body is recalled
to itself, and to its own deepest knowledge. 'The old human
body is the same as it always was,' Lewis says. 'It still feels that
old fear, and that old pain.' (p. 50) Both these feelings can lead to
a man's deliverance. 'I felt wonderful,' Ed says on the cliff-side,
'and fear was at the center of the feeling.' (pp. 171–2) Pain, we
have already seen, can be equated to freedom itself.

If this is what Ed learns from pain, Lewis learns something too.
Lying with a badly broken leg at the bottom of a canoe, he is
dropped over a falls. Afterwards he says, 'I felt it in my leg, and I
tell you, I know something I didn't know before.' (p. 230) What
that something is he doesn't explain, but we sense it in Ed's
assessment of Lewis after their return: 'He has changed, too, but
not in obvious ways. He can die now; he knows that dying is
better than immortality.' (p. 277) What this means is that Lewis
has relinquished his push for survival, along with his claims to
final control. At the book's opening his hand hovering over the
map 'seemed to have power over the terrain, and when it stopped for Lewis's voice to explain something, it was as though all
streams everywhere quit running, hanging silently where they
were to let the point be made.' Now Lewis knows that power
runs with the river.

Ed has learned that lesson too; and both men bring this inex-
pressible knowledge back to the civilization they left. Yet it is not
a knowledge sanctioned by their society, or seen as providing
boons for it; indeed it is the very antithesis of society's image of
itself as one 'whose habitation is high'. So not only the facts of the
killings but the deep knowledge gained through them remain
secret, buried under deep waters. The men do not return as
heroes – far from it. One member of their party has been killed on

the river; and at the news his stunned wife can only say over and over again how 'useless' the whole trip was. If Ed and Lewis have gained their manhood, they are certainly not recognized for it. As society judges these things, Lewis would probably be considered more manly before, in his macho postures of domination, than he is after he has acquired a deeper knowledge. What has happened is that these men have realized their masculine archetype, and in the very act of realizing it have relinquished it. Their mythic experience has ended not by creating the hero but by disabusing men of their heroic self-concept: this may be the truest realization of manhood.

In its way, Robert F. Jones's *Blood Sport* is also about realizing and relinquishing an archetypal manhood. The sport of the title is of course the hunt. This hunt takes place on the Hassayampa, a mythical river which empties into a lake in New York state, and rises in the Altyn Tagh mountain range in Northern China. To go up this river is to go back into time, and even out of time: the game on its banks includes mastodons, Viet Cong, and unicorns. Jones has a dazzling, quirky imagination, which he has the courage to push to the point of silliness. An idea of his gifts may be gotten from a fishing interlude early in the book. Worms do not work for this part of the river, so a special lure is needed:

> an electric-blue Camaro Z-28 with a gold racing stripe, B.F. Goodrich steel-belted street radials, an STP sticker on the right rear windshield, and a pimply blond teen-age driver in a T-shirt that read SHYTTE in Old English script, the whole lure measuring only two inches in length and weighing three quarters of an ounce, exclusive of the stainless-steel treble hooks that dangled fore and aft. (p. 53)

The lure is cast and then pulled in at top speed while the squeal of tyres is faintly heard underwater. As the lure is suddenly let sink there is a tremendous crash and a Plymouth Fury II squad car is brought up. Since it is, regrettably, empty ('the two cops had already split') a Yellow Cab lure is used; and it comes up with several pedestrians which can then be dressed out and cooked. Aside from the comic aspects, this has the effect of correlating one blood sport with another. In the world of the Hassayampa, it is not discovered that men may be killed as trophies but assumed: Mao Mao are brought home on car fenders. This rich and bizarre

world is presided over by an elusive presence known as Ratnose. The one-eyed leader of a robber band, he is intelligent to a
degree matched only by his cruelty.

In Jones's novel, as in Mailer's, a father and son go on a hunting
expedition together; and here too Oedipal tensions erupt. There
are no signs of such tensions in the first part of the book, which is
narrated by the father. He is only concerned that his son might be
a bit of a sissy, and for that reason feels the trip will be good for
him. However, after some weeks the son takes off on his own,
disgusted because he assumes his father has been too soft-
hearted to kill a prisoner they've taken. As the son picks up the
narration we wonder if his father ever knew him. He has gone to
join Ratnose's outlaw band because 'he was rotten to the core and
frankly I'd always suspected that I was that way too.' (p. 106)
When he finds the band, he undergoes a series of tests by way of
initiation. Once accepted, he goes through dramatic changes,
living in a macho fantasy world of primitive violence and sex.
These changes, though, may not be as total as they seem; for the
runaway boy – or Runner, as he is now called – begins to enact an
Oedipal rivalry with Ratnose. He covets Ratnose's woman, and
when he does get her, has her in the same rear-entry posture he
once watched his rival perform, exulting that 'I was Ratnose!'
Ratnose himself is aware of these dynamics, at one point finding
it 'interesting that you should compare me to your father'. (p.
193) According to a thirteenth-century Dominican friar who was
unfortunate enough to fall into his hands, Ratnose is particularly
fond of manipulating the Oedipal patterns: 'he delighteth in
perverting the young to his wicked ways, pitting them soul to
soul against their elders, so that finally the young destroy their
loving parents . . . mutilating them in heart and limb alike . . .
while their new satanic master laugheth with wicked glee.' (p.
66)

Ratnose gets his chance to indulge these tastes when Runner's
father turns up again – but maddened by his son's loss, and
metamorphosed. He has become Tilkut, the bear god, killing and
mutilating all he encounters. With the bearskin that he wears
he has assumed that animal's power. As in Dickey, though, a
creature is released that had always been contained inside; for in
an early encounter with a bear, Runner had heard from it 'a low,
sorrowful moaning up and down, like my father sometimes

makes in his sleep when he isn't snoring'. (p. 108) When the father is finally captured (by the son), Ratnose has a proposal: he and Tilkut will fight a duel, of a most ingenious sort. Where the Hassa and the Yampa join to form the great river there is a mile-deep whirlpool known as the Suck Hole. The two men will stand on the water on either side of this, armed only with fishing rods. Each will try to hook the other with a poisoned fly and drag him into the whirlpool. Both of the boy's Oedipal rivals thus in their turn become rivals, by now with the stature of comic-book superheroes. Though hooked in the leg himself, Tilkut manages to hook Ratnose into the Suck Hole. Father and son make their getaway then, and return from their hunting trip.

As far as their masculine values go, the contest between Tilkut and Ratnose may seem like that between Tweedledum and Tweedledee. In the boy's mind, however, as he waits for the appointed day, the conflict between the two men becomes one between two types of men; and 'he could not decide which man he wished to become.' (p. 220) Meanwhile, the two types of men are amicably tying their flies together while arguing over life styles. The boy's father has the last word: at home, his son will

> play at power and at love – subtle games, full of machinations, maybe, but the kind of play that can turn him into something more than a mere killer and fucker. Your way of life, with its orgies of blood and sex, seems free at first glance – captivating, even – but it produces simple machines. That's why I'm going to kill you and bring my son out of it. (p. 218)

As in Marlowe's *Tamburlaine*, he who wins the argument wins the battle. Macho values themselves are not called into question here: the debate is between simple and complex versions as they are found in the world of the hunt and in civilization. The dichotomy is not really as clear-cut as it is made to seem; for the 'simple' life is so only if one thinks simply about it, and the 'complex' life has underneath it simple and archetypal patterns.

In the end, the son chooses the father's world – or rather, he allows that choice to be made for him by circumstances. In this, Runner is not so different from D.J. and Tex. Though on the surface they appear to be self-directed, a second look at almost every move they make finds there the very pattern they are trying to escape. When the boys break away from the rest of the expedition, they are only re-enacting Rusty's earlier decision to split off on his own with D.J. in search of grizzly. The boys' motive now is that they are sick of this technological, helicopter-aided hunting; but what they are embarking on in Vietnam is only another version of the same. What has been revealed to them is the 'will to kill' – but whose will? If it is that of nature red in tooth and claw, then the question of the book's title gets a terrible answer; we are in Vietnam because it is natural, inevitable, and therefore right that men should kill. But another interpretation is possible if we recall the book's notion of dreams as radio waves; for 'all the messages of North America go up to the Brooks Range. That land above the circle, man, is the land of the icy wilderness and the lost peaks and the unseen deeps and the spires, crystal receiver of the continent.' (p. 172) What it is receiving, then, and transmitting to the boys is the will of their country's unconscious. The boys take on as their own an American dream, or nightmare. Finally, the very fact that they are obeying a command like 'Fulfill my will' clearly indicates that all their activity is actually passive. The only choice they make is to lose themselves in another's will. In both Mailer's books and Jones's, a son consciously or unconsciously chooses his father's world. An Oedipal ambivalence is acted out: the rebellion from the father is at the same time a desire to replace him, to become him. Disguised though it may sometimes be, the role the son inherits is the one that he initially resisted.

It is not so easy, then, to relinquish the masculine myth; it has an enduring power. In *Blood Sport* this is brought home by a one-page epilogue. We see Ratnose's henchman squatting by the Hassayampa river, where he has been waiting a long time. The current sweeps along its usual motley flotsam. Finally he sees what he has been looking for: the naked, broken body of a man. He drags it to shore and carefully arranges its limbs. He sits back on his heels and waits. There is a flicker of movement; the chest rises and falls. Then the one eye opens. Plainly the idea is to leave the reader with a final *frisson*. But given the book's pre-occupations, another idea is implied as well. Those who feel that they have escaped the masculine myth, or mastered it, or trans-cended it, are only deceiving themselves; they are still in the trap which Ratnose personifies. '*I* am the trapper,' he says. 'Not of mere animals, but of men, Runner, of men and boys. I bait my traps with the two most effective lures known to man – curiosity and challenge. No man can resist the chance of knowledge or the threat of death.' (p. 193) These two things are precisely what the initiation rite offers; and they are not likely to lose their allure. We remember, with Ed Gentry, that boys are always looking for ways to become men.

At one point in *Deliverance* Ed accuses his macho friend Lewis of having only a fantasy life. Lewis replies, 'That's all anybody has got. It depends on how strong your fantasy is, and whether you really – *really* – in your own mind, measure up to what you've fantasized.' (p. 49) As we have seen, *Deliverance* is largely about the process by which a man learns to measure up to his fantasies and to realize them. All three of these books could be described as male fantasies in the popular sense of that word. But in their differing degrees – ranging from Dickey to the extravagant Jones – they also have much in common with the literary mode of fantasy. In *Fantasy: The Literature of Subversion* Rosemary Jackson has tried to present a consensus of opinion about this elusive mode. 'The fantastic,' she says, 'traces the unsaid and unseen of culture: that which has been silenced, made invisible, covered over and made "absent" '.[8] In the case of these books a masculine ideology has been extended until it ends in the acting out of forbidden desires. Fantasy's relation to desire is twofold, Jackson tells us: 'it can *tell of*, manifest or show desire . . . or it can *expel* desire. . . . In many cases fantastic literature fulfils both functions at once.'[9] One word describes such a dual function: this literature *expresses* desire, both in the usual sense of manifesting it, and in its literal sense of pressing out, and so expelling. There is always a question, however, as to how much can be expressed in either sense; and it is a question particularly apt to these three novels. The hero-hunter, according to Jameson, brings back with him 'a story which can never be told'. If his new knowledge is by definition uncommunicable, that is because it is largely body-knowledge, which – as Mishima would stress – is the very opposite of words. The primitive nature of that knowledge leads to a paradox: that the underside of a society, its 'unsaid and unseen', is in a novel expressed in the language of that society. 'Telling,' Jackson says, 'implies using the language of the dominant order and so accepting its norms, recovering its dark areas.'[10]

The tension being described echoes a familiar one, that between language and a certain kind of masculinity. In one way, as Jameson puts it, 'the writing of the novel is the first arena in which you prove your manhood, in which you show whether you are really capable of appropriating the social totality itself, in the way a businessman appropriates it when, by making his million, he shows that he knows the facts of life of that otherwise "untotalizable totality" which is America today.'[11] On the other hand, all this amounts to is becoming a man like Rusty Jethroe – in D.J.'s language, a High Grade Asshole. The whole of Mailer's novel describes the search for another kind of manhood, even if that search does become futile and delusive in the end – and the same is true of the other two novels.[12] Language then becomes the final betrayal of what these men have been looking for all along. For such reasons, men attempting to find the words to measure up to their fantasies should find themselves sharing some of Anna Dawe's wariness. They should distrust 'the curious little narrative tricks' because they are tricks of the trade, part of the business of writing like an H.G.A. And they should distrust that omniscience that Anna Dawe finds so typically male, because they have been initiated into another kind of male knowledge, of that which is an absence. Dickey, Mailer and Jones all evince this kind of distrust – but in varying degrees and only up to a point.

Instead of having an omniscient narrator, all three novels are narrated in the first person. We are not allowed to forget that what we are experiencing is being told, that there is a teller. What we *are* allowed to forget, often, is why the telling is taking place at all – the teller's motives, and his relation to the experience of telling. Dickey's Ed Gentry never begins to raise such questions; so of the three books, *Deliverance* represents the novel in its most monological form. This, according to Bakhtin, is the form which the novel had on its emergence, implicitly claiming that 'all that has significance can be collected in a single consciousness and subordinated to a single accent; everything which is not amenable to such reduction is accidental and unessential.'[13] An ostentatious pulling away from such a form is found in *Why Are We in Vietnam*? For one thing, a question is raised as to whether, or how, the narrator really exists. Perhaps, we are told, there is no such person as D.J. and we are being put on by a black 'genius brain up in Harlem'. But this claim is a teasing put-on; rather than a serious questioning of convention, it is a reflection of Mailer's fondness for competition, for squaring off even against his readers. Similarly, when it is suggested that the book is a tape-recording of D.J.'s brain or an emanation of his electro-magnetic waves, this is merely McLuhanesque window-dressing. Totally ignored are questions of how these emanations end up as a linear medium. Ignored also are D.J.'s direct addresses to the reader, like 'New concept, Suckmouth!' These are only updated versions of eighteenth-century addresses to the 'gentle reader'. The novel is not only a monologue – 'stream of conch', D.J. calls it – it is far more monological in form than its ostensible differences would lead us to expect. A more conventional-seeming novel, *Blood Sport* attains a more dialogical complexity. Though it gives no probing or even plausible explanation of the motive for writing, the novel fractures its narrative point of view in significant ways. The narration is split, as we have seen, between father and son. When it shifts back, it appears to be returning to the father in a first-person account headed 'Tilkut's irrationale'. But that is only one exhibit among several assembled by an omniscient tale-teller. Entering now at will into the consciousness of father or son, or evaporating point of view altogether in a dramatized section, the author ends with a detached rendition of Ratnose's resurrection which emphasizes its mythic quality. In its texture as well as its structure, this novel fulfils a major criterion for the fantastic: that it set up a dialogue both with reality and with literature.

Mailer questions literature at one point of his novel by observing 'It's a wise man who knows he is the one doing the writer's writing.' (p. 28) For him, writing is a kind of underground journey in which the 'fabulous forces' encountered are those of other possible selves, leaping into febrile, fantastic life. This is so for all three of these authors, though each conveys it by his own image. In *Why Are We in Vietnam?* the image is that of a radio crystal which is simultaneously the icy cap of the Arctic circle and the mind of the narrator; and what this crystal transmits are the electro-magnetic waves of the unconscious, that part which is hidden from 'the world of common day':

when you go into sleep, that mind of yours leaps, stirs, and

> sifts itself into the Magnetic-Electro fief of the dream . . . you
> are a part of the spook flux of the night like an iron filing in the
> E.M. field. . . . (p. 170)

That sense of flux is the distinctive quality of Mailer's whole
novel. In *Deliverance* the central image is that of the river, so
strongly identified with sleep and the unconscious when Ed
Gentry first launches out on it. When Ed returns from his
journey, he is changed in many ways; and one of the most
significant is that he has moved beyond being a merely compe-
tent graphic designer and is now something of an artist. He
knows why this is so: 'The river underlies, one way or another,
everything I do.' (p. 257) It is Dickey's artistry as well that makes
this admission. The river in *Blood Sport* functions in a similar way.
The peculiar properties of the Hassayampa are the source of the
whole book. To journey up this river is to journey into the
unconscious, to the very headwaters of fantasy.

The epigraph to *Blood Sport* purports to be a quote from one
Sparse Grey Hackle: 'Just as the water of the famed Hassayampa
renders those who drink it incapable of telling the truth. . . .'
There is a reminiscence here of the tall-tale-telling of hunters and
fishermen. More important, though, is the frank admission that
the whole book is a tissue of lies. This does not invalidate its
status as a masculine truth; paradoxically, it confers still more
status upon it. One of Ratnose's favourite sayings is this: 'To
ride, shoot straight and tell a lie is all you need to teach a guy.' (p.
138). The reason that lying is included in this list has best been
expressed by Mailer: 'There is hardly a guy alive who is not an
actor to the hilt – for the simplest of reasons. He cannot be tough
all the time . . . so he acts to fill the gap. A comedy of adopted
manners surrounds the probing each tough guy is forever giving
his brother.'[14] As we have seen, a man who begins by acting a role
for the benefit of others or himself may end by acting out a reality:
true change begins with a lie. An outrageous episode like fishing
with car lures invites our admiration for the same reasons that
Mailer's surrealistic bravado does. It is an act of daring; an un-
ashamed lie is pushed through by sheer bullish energy. It then
becomes more than a lie – it becomes fantasy.

Two kinds of fantasy have been dealt with here: fantasy as a
literary genre, and fantasy as an activity of the psyche. The two

are united in what Robert Kroetsch calls 'the tell-tale self'. This is a self that one should both suspect and celebrate. On the one hand, fantasy can initiate change through its connection to the unconscious. It is a crack in reality through which pour in rich tumult those things that are excluded by society and therefore the ones that can renew it. On the other hand, fantasy may also be an exaggerated parallel to society's values – not challenging them, but corroborating them. So D.J.'s mystical hunting experience is itself a kind of fantasy which replays the macho preoccupations of his father in another key; inevitably this leads him to Vietnam, the dark unconscious of the American Dream. In this kind of fantasy, one is initiated only into the existing social order. Like the knowledge offered by Ratnose's world, fantasy may free us or trap us – sometimes trapping us exactly when we feel most free. Fantasy is a double-edged instrument of change, corresponding to that 'region of supernatural wonder' in which the hero undergoes his initiation. However, if real boons are to be brought back from the experience, a real testing must take place in that fantasy: fantasy must question reality. Where literary fantasies of manhood are concerned, this means that the text should not be monologically masculine but polyphonic, flexible enough to include its opposite. The 'daylight' idea of manhood must be tested too, must even risk dying. To do anything else would be to affirm only a boy's idea of manhood. To the boy, manhood seems at the same time mysterious and simple: it is something one can achieve by certain acts, be initiated into at a certain time and place. But the man knows that initiation takes longer. One is introduced to that inner realm of fabulous forces, but one does not pass through it, conquering it once and for all. In all three of the novels dealt with here, the initiation is open-ended; and all three question the idea of manhood even while they affirm it. To such fantasies as these we can trust ourselves, if we can trust ourselves at all. Where manhood is concerned it is most advisable – indeed, most manly – to be alert. Yielding to an over-easy nostalgia makes for a flabby mind. However reluctantly, men today must face up to the full implications of Mailer's warning that to assume manhood too readily is to lose some of it.

CHAPTER 7

Supermale

If the hero, as indicated in the last chapter, embodies certain masculine expectations, we can learn yet more about masculinity by turning our attention to the extreme version of the hero: the 'superhero', as he is now referred to in the comic-book trade. The definitive comic-book superhero was conceived in 1933 by two seventeen-year-old boys. Superman is that to which every man aspires. It isn't only that he is stronger than anyone else around, or that he leads a life full of action and adventure. Superman also fulfils less obvious requirements of masculine role-playing – the need for success, for instance. Despite any temporary setbacks, Superman is always and undoubtedly 'number one' – a phrase that is increasingly becoming associated with the *macho* stance. Superman attains this success not by playing a role, but merely by being what he is. In him there is a reversal of Robert Graves's dubious dictum that 'Men do; women are.' Superman 'does', all right, but that is a natural consequence of what he is. There is no existential need for him to prove his manhood through a series of actions, as there is for one enacting the usual masculine roles, such as hunter or soldier. The only role-playing that is done is the pretence that he is *less* than he is: that he is mild-mannered Clark Kent. The role of Clark Kent is an entirely unnecessary one from the practical point of view – something of a waste of Superman's time. However, Clark Kent is psychologically necessary because in his very ordinariness he represents the reader. The reader of superhero comics – almost invariably male – is like Clark Kent in being a creature of compromises and failures, whose energies are sapped by daily life. He takes comfort, though, from the suggestion that this is merely a temporary role. His real identity is within him, an inviolable core of pure masculinity. That vaguely sensed core is incarnated for him in Superman.

Of course there have been superheroes long before 1933, and for many of these same reasons. As one comic-book critic points out,

> . . . the crew of Jason's ship, the *Argo*, was made up largely of heroes who had most of Superman's powers among them. Besides Herakles, there were Zetes and Kalais, who flew; Euphemos, the super-speedster; Kaineus, who was invulnerable; and even Lynkeus, who, we are told, could see things underground – yes, X-ray vision, in ancient Greece![1]

Jason, along with Perseus, Theseus, Zeus and Apollo, defeats a dragon-like antagonist who is seen by Joseph Campbell as a relic of the 'serpent consort' important to a matriarchal theology. These superheroes represent the new patriarchal values; they are models not only for individual men but for whole civiliza- tions.[2] I do not wish, however, to go so far back nor to take so wide a view of the superhero. Instead, I will deal here with one of Superman's twentieth-century predecessors. He appears in a short novel called *The Supermale (Le Surmâle)*, written in 1902 by Alfred Jarry.

Only by the science which he himself invented can Alfred Jarry be defined. For one of the purposes of 'Pataphysics is to examine the laws governing exceptions, and Jarry has a good claim to being the most exceptional man who ever lived. All the ordinary conventions of existence were flouted by a man who saw life itself as a strange and temporary conjunction; who defined the universe as 'that which is the exception to oneself'; and who scrawled these words at the end of his most compre- hensive work, *The Life and Opinions of Doctor Faustroll, 'Pataphy- sician*: 'This book will only be published as a whole when the author has acquired enough experiences to savor all its beauties.' The book was published in 1911, four years after his death. He had a notion that the brain continued to dream after death, and that the dreams produced by its gradual dissolution were the source of the idea of paradise. In his own life he did his best to bring that paradise to earth. The stories told about Jarry all have a dream-like absurdity about them: he would appear wearing a fur tiara or a tie painted on his shirtfront; he shared his room with owls and chameleons; his dying request was for a toothpick. It may seem rather inadequate, then, to propose the investigation of Jarry using as clue his sex – our sex being that which, after life itself, is the first limitation of our possible experience.

Still, Jarry's sexuality is worth investigation in its own right, and plays its part in his written works. As a mere schoolboy he appears to have frequented brothels. But 'we do not like women at all,' Jarry asserted, referring to himself in the royal plural.[3] Some have seen in him a submerged homosexuality. He visited the theatre several times in the company of Lord Douglas, the notorious friend of Oscar Wilde; and he wrote of homosexual love in *Haldernablou*, an early work. There the homosexual protagonist muses: 'I would like someone who was neither man, nor woman, nor altogether monster, a devoted slave who could speak without breaking the harmony of my sublime thoughts. . . .'[4] It appears that Jarry too is unwilling to incarnate himself in a sexual love of any kind which might distract him from his narcissistic self-absorption. So the sexuality which is present in his works is generally symbolical, a stance of the mind rather than of the body. The phallic symbol, for instance, appears repeatedly. In the prologue to *Haldernablou* a sacred phallus destroys a crumbling temple; the apocalypse near the end of *Faustroll* is described in terms of an ejaculation. Apollinaire, after describing Jarry's low-ceilinged room as 'filled with reductions', tells us of the one apparent exception to this rule:

> On the mantel stood a large stone phallus, a gift from Félicien Rops. Jarry kept this member, which was considerably larger than life size, always covered with a violet skull-cap of velvet, ever since the day the exotic monolith had frightened a certain literary lady who was all out of breath from climbing three and a half floors and at a loss how to act in this unfurnished cell.
> 'Is that a cast?' the lady asked.
> 'No,' said Jarry. 'It's a reduction.'[5]

Jarry's use of masculinity, and his insights into it, are found most of all in *The Supermale*.[6] The novel opens at a fashionable *soirée* with an assertion that the act of love can be performed an indefinite number of times in succession. Andre Marcueil, who makes this statement, appears the least likely man to arrive at this conclusion through experience, being built along the lines of

Charlie Chaplin, Woody Allen, or the five-foot-high Jarry himself. As scholarly proof he cites the case of an Indian 'celebrated by Theophrastus' who in one day performed the act seventy times. Nobody credits this. Only a young girl named Ellen believes in the Indian – and in Marcueil. Ellen is the daughter of an American chemist who is about to prove the validity of his new 'Perpetual Motion Food' by racing a five-man bicycle team against an express train for a course of ten thousand miles. Marcueil on his own bicycle shadows the five-man team. He has sufficient leisure during the night to cover with roses the railway car in which Ellen is riding. Only Ellen seems to realize that the mysterious rider who shadows the race is Marcueil giving, as it were, a preliminary demonstration of his super-virile powers. He next produces, for a selected party of witnesses, an 'Indian' – actually Marcueil himself in red paint – who is going to attempt to break the previous record. Ellen, getting wind of the plan, locks in a room the five prostitutes who have been obtained for the occasion. Masked, she takes the place of all of them. The record is broken, but so is Ellen. Just as Marcueil realizes the depth of his love for her he discovers that she is apparently dead. It is only 'apparently', however: Ellen later recovers with little effort. Marcueil, unfortunately, does not. In a state of shock he is seized by Ellen's father and hooked up to a new invention – a machine-to-inspire-love. This is with some idea of saving his daughter's honour, and with no notion that Marcueil already loves Ellen. The machine backfires and electrocutes the Supermale. As for Ellen, she consoles herself with a more ordinary husband.

Part of the charm of Jarry's novel for today's readers is its period décor – though it is difficult to say exactly what period is being evoked. Numerous details plainly belong to the world of 1902: the moustaches and pince-nez, trailing skirts, bicycles and motoring goggles. Yet we are told that the events of the book take place in 1920. Jarry has then given us more than the 'modern novel' which his subtitle promises. He has given us a futuristic one along the lines of Jules Verne, one of his favourite authors. Of course the 'futuristic' date of 1920 now elicits only nostalgia from the reader. The passage of time itself, then, has made of *The Supermale* a paradox in time, one which renders it impossible for the reader to settle into standard attitudes towards past and future. It is exactly the kind of temporal paradox that Jarry liked.

Above all, though, *The Supermale* is a myth of masculinity which, as a myth, has a validity beyond its historical period. I have mentioned Jules Verne, whose myth expresses the eventual redemption of man through machinery. Jarry often expresses something similar, revelling in the release of human potential made possible by the new inventions of 1920. At the same time he appears to be expressing a counter-myth: that of man *versus* machine. For all its use of the new 'Perpetual Motion Food', the five-man bicycle team is obviously pitting its human capacities against the mechanical ones of the locomotive. André Marcueil challenges the dynamometer, a carnival machine to measure strength, with the express intention of 'killing' it; and he does. He is himself killed by a stronger machine, the machine-to-inspire-love. It is significant that both of these machines are characterized as female. The vertical coin slot of the dynamo-meter provokes Marcueil's comment that 'It's a female . . . but a very strong one.' And the machine-to-inspire-love first falls in love with the man and then destroys him, in a hideous parody of the sexual 'electricity' between man and woman. It is more exact, then, to speak of the theme of *male* versus machine. But beyond that, and at the core of Jarry's myth, is the idea of male *as* machine.

It is the witness to Marcueil's sexual marathon who first explicitly asserts that 'He's not a man, he's a machine.' This comment suggests the construction and use of a machine-to-inspire-love.

> If André Marcueil were a machine . . . the combined efforts of the engineer, the chemist and the physician would pit one machine against another for the greater good of bourgeois science, medicine and morality. Since this man had become a mechanism, the equilibrium of the world required that another mechanism should manufacture – a soul. (p. 77)

The plan backfires, however, and for purely mechanical reasons. 'Everyone knows that when two electro-dynamic machines are coupled together, the one with the higher output charges the other.' (p. 79) Consequently the machine-to-inspire-love itself falls in love with the man-machine. Even before this 'scientific' proof, of course, the notion of Marcueil as machine has been strongly implied – most interestingly in the stress on breaking records. For 'a soul' is just what is irrelevant in record-breaking. It is not some psychological quality that matters, but sheer mathematical quantity. At the conclusion of Marcueil's sexual marathon we are told that 'assiduous love-making leaves no time to experience love'. (p. 71) Only when the record is broken does Marcueil discover his love for Ellen. But what is the nature of this love? It too turns out to be curiously mechanical.

The nature of love is a topic much discussed by Marcueil's guests in the opening scene of the novel. Love as a sentiment is played down in favour of Marcueil's more provocative suggestions. He feels that love is 'an attenuated act, most likely; that is, not quite an act; or better still, a potential act'. (p. 3) The logical objection is raised by one guest: would the completed act then exclude love? Marcueil's reply indicates that one act may always be followed by another; and the stirrings of that potential act are what he would call love. There is simply no such thing as a completed act. The acts of love are infinite to the man who is a 'sex machine' of the type so energetically celebrated by rock singer James Brown. Now, if love is only an interval of potentiality between two actualities, those intervals will have to be very short when you are out to break a sexual record and are operating under a time limit. Thus Marcueil in his marathon has 'no time to experience love'.

The whole marathon is proof of Marcueil's theories, but given a fatal twist with himself as victim. Marcueil, who is described as a machine, is also in a special sense of the word romantic: he constantly aspires towards the infinite and must therefore remain constantly unfulfilled. In his case, of course, the infinity is one of physical acts. But only a Supermale is capable of enduring an infinity of such acts. For others, inevitably, 'there was an end.' At the end of their love-making, Ellen lies across the bed, to all appearances a corpse. In the realization of one of the commonest male fantasies, she has literally been 'fucked to death'. Her death has an extraordinary effect on the Supermale; and it is nothing so simple as remorse. To begin with, we are told, 'He would never have seen her, if she had not been dead.' (p. 70) Now he sees, as if for the first time, all the features of her face and body. He kisses them – 'a thing he had not previously thought of doing, imagining that it would be evidence of a momentary impotence where more virile caresses were concerned.' (p. 71) Finally he realizes and admits to himself that he is in love with Ellen. If we apply Marcueil's own theories of love here, we see what has occurred. Ellen is dead, he thinks. So the stirrings of yet another sexual act have no possibility for actualization, but must remain forever potential. And love is precisely that interval of potential action, now become a permanent state.

Death does not only mean the removal to a realm of unfulfilled potential, though. It is also the removal to a realm beyond the human, and the result may be a superhuman intensity. A purely physical example is provided earlier in the book by the case of Jewey Jacobs, a member of the five-man bicycle team. Midway in the race he dies of exhaustion, though he is still locked into the bicycle. The corpse's inertia is, with effort, overcome. Then the corpse begins to act like a flywheel; its pedalling speed catches up with that of the rest of the team; and finally 'not only did he catch up with us, but he increased his speed beyond ours, and Jacob's death-sprint was a sprint the like of which the living cannot conceive.' (p. 35) The episode points towards a fundamental tenet in Jarry: that always beyond the limited capacities of the living are infinite and absolute forces which fully reveal themselves only to the dead – or the not yet born. So the new born baby is 'a little, pale-coral Buddha, hiding its eyes, which are so dazzled by their proximity to the absolute that they have never opened, hiding its eyes behind its little star-like hand. . . .' (p. 56) No less than birth and death, copulation borders on the absolute. Copulation on such a grand and intense scale as Marcueil's has been nothing less than an attempt to break through the limits of human capacity, to batter down the doors of the absolute.

In the infinite abysses of the human body, says Jarry, dwell the spermatozoa and the ova like millions of gods and goddesses. They govern man tyrannically – until a superman, like Marcueil, rises like a titan against them. His goal is to attain the absolute and to establish himself as the new god. Ellen intuitively understands this, and it colours her remarks in an early conversation with Marcueil. 'The Absolute Lover must exist, since woman can conceive of him,' she asserts. And she goes on: 'I believe in him because no one else will . . . *because it is absurd* . . . as I believe in

God!' (pp. 26–7) And Marcueil does attain to his goal of the absolute, but by two routes at once. Ellen's death is almost as instrumental as his own sexuality. Sexually he has at last reached fulfilment: '. . . Marcueil perceived that at this stage of his spent energies, when another man would have been fatigued, he was becoming sentimental. This was his transformation of the *post coitum animal triste*.' (p. 72) And Ellen's death not only evokes love, for the reasons given above; it also evokes a kind of sympathetic following of her into the realm of death. Marcueil muses on

> her light, delicate, and perfumed memory, her floating and delicious living image, almost more delicious than her living form itself. For I am sure she will never leave me, and it is only the desire for an unattainable eternity that obsesses and spoils the ephemeral joys of lovers. (p. 75)

Marcueil has attained that unattainable eternity.

Immediately after his own realization of this fact, Marcueil is seen to ignore a number of things which would ordinarily be very hard to ignore. Ellen revives, gets up and goes home; and her indignant father has Marcueil wired to the machine-to-inspire-love. Marcueil's obliviousness of both events is only explained by the fact, mentioned in passing, that he is 'still plunged in a stupor'. Plainly this is not just a sexual stupor; more likely it is the stupor of love; but most of all it must be that Marcueil is still on the *other side* – in that hallucinatory realm which Jarry viewed as more real than the world of the living. The imagery itself at this point indicates that Marcueil has attained his eternity, has achieved his godhead at the same moment that he is about to meet his martyrdom.

> The doctor, Arthur Gough, and William Elson were observing, unseen, from the neighboring room, and the patient with his [electrical] crown, still undressed, and with his make-up peeling off in places, as the gilding wears off a statue, presented so inhuman a spectacle that the two Americans, who 'knew their Gospels,' needed a few moments to compose themselves and call on their common sense to shake off the pitiful and supernatural image of the King of the Jews diademed with thorns and nailed on a cross. (p. 78)

Nevertheless, the scientists persist in their experiment, with the results we already know. Marcueil's tragedy is – rather like Christ's – to be the victim of his own incarnation. That aspect of him which is his godhead leads to a deceptive mildness which is really an indifference to the events of time on the part of one preoccupied with eternity. He therefore falls victim to the creatures of time.

For all the connections with Jarry's hallucinatory mysticism, though, the tragic flaw of this particular hero is still love. In *L'amour absolu*, Jarry refers to 'the dregs of Love which is Fear',[7] and we have seen the phrase justified here. The Supermale is the most remarkable of 1920s remarkable machines; but when that machine falls in love it falls once and for all into society's hands. It is then Woman above all who must be feared by a Supermale, or by anyone aspiring to become one. Ellen at first appears to be destroyed by Marcueil; but ultimately it is she who destroys him. In a long poetic reverie he names Ellen rightly as Helen, destroyer of men. It is Ellen who, consciously or not, wills that the Supermale pass beyond the mechanical to love. She visits Marcueil in his lodgings for no other purpose than to assure him of her faith in the Absolute Lover. She locks the doxies up in a gallery and singlehandedly takes their place. 'I love him,' she replies to her father's questioning, adding nothing more useful to prevent the tragic finale. Her instincts are set on an Absolute Lover – but only so that she may bind him by love. It is a common enough view of what women want.

This view is also that of George Bernard Shaw, whose *Man and Superman* was written at exactly the same time as Jarry's work. A comparison with Shaw's play brings out more clearly some of the submerged elements in *The Supermale*. Foremost among these is the Nietzschean element. At the Lycée Henri IV Jarry and his classmates were lectured by Professor Bourdon on the philosophy of Nietzsche well before his works were translated into French. 1900, the year of Nietzsche's death, had witnessed a tremendous upsurge of interest in his writings – so much so that, as Shaw observes, people tended to 'chatter harmlessly' about him as a fashionable topic. His philosophy must have been a congenial one to Jarry, for Nietzschean strains are woven throughout the body of his work: the idea that the living being is only a rare variant of the dead one; the scorn for the crowd expressed by an assertion of intense individuality; the idea that man himself must replace his dead god. In *The Supermale* there is always a pushing past the supposed limits of human capacities, a straining into the yet unrealized future. Jarry comments casually on the endless driveways of Marcueil's chateau, built in the reign of Louis XVIII. It almost seems as if these were not merely built 'for carriages to creep on, but that the architect, by some obscure premonitory flash of genius, had designed them, three hundred years in advance, for modern vehicles'. And he goes on to generalize: 'There is certainly no reason for men to build enduring works if they do not vaguely imagine that these works must wait for some additional beauty with which they themselves cannot invest them, but which the future holds in store.' (p. 15) The Nietzschean Superman appears in many guises in Jarry's work. Dr Faustroll enacts the impulse as a voyager in strange seas of thought; Ubu expresses a vital anarchic crudeness; Marcueil enacts the role in terms of masculinity.

Both Jarry and Shaw use one of the commonest masculine myths, that of Don Juan, transforming it to suit their own purposes. In Jarry's case Don Juan is born, so to speak, from his female counterpart. *Messalina*, written a year before *The Supermale*, celebrates the lascivious wife of the Emperor Claudius and relates the events leading to her death by the sword – which Messalina's imagination transforms into the apotheosis of phallus. It seems that she too is enamoured of sexual statistics: she engages in a copulation contest and exhausts twenty-four men in as many hours. Jarry comments, 'A man is Messalina's husband during the moment of love, and then for an indefinite period of time, given only that he be capable of living an uninterrupted series of moments of love.'[8] The Supermale is that man; and he cites Messalina herself as evidence that human capacities are limitless. Yet the Don Juanism of both the man and the woman represents an aspiration which is more than just sexual. Shaw explains it all, as he is so fond of doing: 'Don Juanism is no longer misunderstood as mere Casanovism,' he says. What is now demanded is 'a Don Juan in the philosophic sense'. And what is that sense?

Philosophically, Don Juan is a man who, though gifted enough to be exceptionally capable of distinguishing between good and evil, follows his own instincts without regard to the common, statute, or canon law: . . . His thousand and three affairs of gallantry . . . have been discarded altogether as unworthy of his philosophic dignity and compromising to his newly acknowledged position as the founder of a school. Instead of pretending to read Ovid he actually does read Schopenhauer and Nietzsche. . . .[9]

And, we may add, preaches a very good Nietzsche in Shaw. In Jarry, the Don Juan figure gives physical expression to his philosophy – not in a thousand and three affairs but in one. One woman is made the new Messalina, and through an act which intensifies at each repetition she attains with him the realm of the super-human.

Beyond Don Juan and the Nietzschean Superman glimmers, dimly, the figure of the Dandy. His is a figure which most people would characterize as effeminate, hardly the supermale type. Aware only that Beau Brummel was preoccupied with clothes, they ignore the nature of those clothes. For velvets, fussy embroidery, frothing lace, Brummel substituted a new restraint, a severity purely masculine: plain starched linen, scrupulously clean; polished boots; subdued colours and precisely elegant tailoring. It is still, basically, the uniform of masculinity today. At the same time he appears to have made fashionable a corresponding restraint in emotion. The nineteenth century, as I have noted, marked a shift from the 'Man of Feeling' to the ideal of a 'stiff upper lip'. Brummel and the line of dandies descended from him played their part in this shift. For the dandy is a mask without a face beneath it. His coruscatingly brilliant wit is always and only of the surface. Yet he is not superficial. A species of Camus's Rebel, he constructs his life over a void. Only personal style, the most tenuous of stuff, accounts for his meaning and his position. By his style, he attains to the pinnacle of society; yet he returns nothing but indifference or scorn to the society whose adulation puts him there. His life is a never-ending work of art. Without the moral earnestness of Nietzsche's superman, he is engaged in creating his own version of the higher type of man.

Dandyism was enjoying one of its intermittent revivals in 1902, and many of Jarry's friends dressed the part. His own clothes were hopeless by any tailor's standard, but in his life no one exhibited more perfectly the philosophy of the dandy. Andre Gide recalls the Jarry of 1905:

> This plaster-faced Kobald, gotten up like a circus clown and acting a fantastic, strenuously contrived role which showed no human characteristic, exercised a remarkable fascination at the Mercure. Almost everyone there attempted, some more successfully than others, to imitate him, to adopt his humor; and above all his bizarre implacable accent – no inflection or nuance and equal stress on every syllable, even the silent ones. A nutcracker, if it could talk, would do no differently.[10]

It is not always easy to distinguish between Jarry's own fabricated personality and the personalities he fabricated in his works. He commonly referred to himself as Ubu, and spoke in Ubu's periphrastic manner. There are indications that he identified himself with the Supermale as well – a character who shares many of Jarry's own interests, such as bicycling. Andre Breton asserted that 'beginning with Jarry, much more than with Wilde, the differentiation long considered necessary between art and life has been challenged, to wind up annihilated as a principle.'[11]

The style of *The Supermale*, too, affects a kind of dandyism: it is urbane, precise, witty, and above all deadpan. The most fantastical events are related with perfect equanimity and self-possession. The narrator wears an impassive mask, just as the dandy does. In writing on the work of Henri de Regnier, Jarry said, 'If the characters show themselves to us behind masks, we must remember that character has no other sense but mask, and that it is the "false face" which is true because personal.'[12] The characters of *The Supermale* mask, under a superficial social identity, an absolute nature which is beyond personality. At times this is stressed by the wearing of actual masks. Ellen visits Marcueil wearing a pink plush driver's mask which she removes with a flourish in anticipation, as it were, of uncovering to Marcueil her real feelings about him. She wears a black mask for the sexual marathon which, significantly, falls off during her apparent death agony. Marcueil's make-up and Indian costume may be seen as a kind of mask – though no more so than the lifelong pretence on his part that he is an ordinary man. When the deadpan mask falls, to be replaced by genuine emotion, then is the moment of Marcueil's downfall, as it is that of the dandy.

Earlier, Jarry has asked, 'Why did Marcueil feel the need at the same time to hide and to reveal himself? To deny his strength and to prove it? In order to test the fit of his mask, no doubt. . . .' (pp. 14–15) The same might be said of the relation of Jarry himself to his writings.

Also present in the style is the hypercivilized aspect of dandyism. The 'smart' setting of the novel's opening is a tissue of fashionable cliches. The guests at Marcueil's *soirée* have a carefully studied variety: besides the American scientists, there is a general, a senator, a baron, a cardinal, a physician, and an actress. Jarry's account of their conversation catches perfectly the rhythm of social badinage. But of course out of these cliches and conventions arises ultimately a staggering refutation of all conventions and their assumed limitations. This too reflects the practice of the dandy: though society is the very atmosphere he breathes, he audaciously turns its conventions against itself. He often carries the expectations of society to such an extreme that they rebound upon themselves in self-parody. In this respect the dandy's role is actually parallel to that of Jarry's supermale. The attributes of masculinity, generally admired and encouraged by society, when taken to their extreme rebound with apocalyptic effect. Only then does society recognize a challenge to its orthodoxy and take steps to punish it.

The dandy has had to update his wardrobe and his wit. Don Juan has left his philosophy books and become a 'swinger'. Only a few Derrideans chatter harmlessly about Nietzsche today. Yet the idea of the supermale remains in the consciousness of people who have never read Jarry. The popularity of superheroes has never been greater. Superman has been followed by a whole host of exotic colleagues: Bullet Man, Plastic Man, the Human Torch, the Incredible Hulk, etc. At the same time the idea of the superhero itself is undergoing change.

The comic-books of the late 1960s saw the rise of the 'superhero with problems'. An example is Spiderman. His distinctive attribute is not so much that he can shoot unbreakable threads out of his fingertips as it is the fact that he is a neurotic and a klutz. What, one wonders, does this do for the reader of *Spiderman*, at present the most popular of the superhero strips? Perhaps it provides the comfort of closer identification in a world where the old ideals of superheroism seem increasingly part of an innocent past. As manhood has become a more complicated business, so its superheroic versions have lost their simple confidence. If Superman is the 'inviolable' core within each man, even that core today faces threats to its continued existence. These threats are reflected in the nature of the problems Superman now faces. No longer are they problems arising from external forces, however ingenious and perverse these might be. Instead they are (or at least are advertised to be) problems that challenge the very possibility of Superman's continued existence in his customary form. On one comic-book cover, the guardians of the universe (who surely should know what they're talking about) convict Superman of 'crimes against humanity'. On another, Clark Kent stalks off, grumbling 'Go find yourself another alter-ego, Superman! I'm tired of being your fall guy!' Superman's existence is obviously more precarious than ever; he is faced with the ever-present possibility of his fall.

In one respect he fell at the very beginning. That is when he decided, in the first issue, to 'turn his titanic strength into channels that would benefit mankind'. For 'mankind' read 'society' of the most conventional kind. Superman has been co-opted by society in a way that spells doom by Nietzsche's standards, or Jarry's, or the dandy's. That version of masculinity which recognizes only its own impulses as laws has had to go underground. We find it in a book like Philip Jose Farmer's *A Feast Unknown*.[13] In this fantasy classic of the 1960s, Tarzan battles Doc Savage – but we are faced with versions of both which are quite different from anything we are used to. Tarzan, we learn, is merely a cleaned-up version of our narrator, who exhibits a benign tolerance for the narrow moral vision of his 'biographer'. Some clue to his own nature is given by the fact that he has an erection at the onset of battle and reaches orgasm when he kills. He is concerned about this phenomenon mostly because the effects of the orgasm incapacitate him for more than one killing. At the end of his adventure he comes to realize that he is being manipulated by those very beings who have given him his superpowers – 'the guardians of the universe', they could be called. And he resolves to liberate himself and the world from their rule. Nothing could be further from the boy-scout aspect of Superman. In Farmer's raw contrary, the superhero regains a virile force akin to that of his turn-of-the-century predecessors. It remains to be seen whether this is the shape of things to come or mere nostalgia for a masculine paradise lost.

CHAPTER 8

The terrain of truth

The image of the bullfight occurs repeatedly among the writers of the School of Virility: Hemingway, Mailer and Mishima are fascinated by it. This is not only because bullfighting is a supremely virile business, but because these authors see it as a metaphor for their own art. The relation between *torero* and bull is an equivalent of the relation between the writer and his masculine subject matter. The bull is of course an essentially phallic figure, a virile ideal. The writer pits himself against this ideal, and by mastering it and controlling it asserts his own virility. To do this he has only words, as slight and even effeminate as the *torero*'s cape. His words, like the cape, can take on a sculptural form, momentary and fluctuating, but with the ability to bring the bull of maleness closer and closer to the author himself. In the end, the *torero* enters the bull's body in an act analogous to sexual penetration. In this way he possesses the bull's virility and asserts his own; if he is unfortunate, the bull's horn impales him. The contest is between two male figures who both seek a phallic triumph. Similarly the author who aspires towards virility in his writing risks, more plainly than other writers, the sense of effeminization if he fails.

The metaphor of the bullfight has been most consciously developed and explored by Michel Leiris. The terms in which he sees the bullfight, however, are not quite the same as those I have just suggested. Leiris's unique interpretation arises from a preoccupation with aesthetics, with autobiography, and above all with his own psychological configuration. Yet in the last analysis Leiris's version of the bullfight metaphor makes a statement on masculinity in general and on certain masculine expectations in the artist. He begins his exploration with *Miroir de la tauromachie*, a short work written in 1937. Here he suggests that real beauty in the bullfight, as elsewhere, partakes of two seemingly opposed elements, which Leiris refers to as the *droit* and the *gauche*: 'On the one hand, *droit*, the element of beauty which is immortal, sovereign, plastic; on the other hand, *gauche*, a sinister element situated on the side of calamity, of accident, of transgression.'[1] In the bull ring, the bull is this *gauche* element, dark and unpredictable. The *torero* is *droit* – the French word's sense of 'law' is reflected in the fact that he, in contrast to the bull, is strictly bound by the rules of the game: his feet must not move during the pass, he must make the bull's whole body pass before his own, and so on. The relation between these two elements in the bullfight, as in all great works of art, is described by Leiris as one of *tangency* – 'the coupling of the straight line with the curved, marriage of the rule and its exception.' He goes on, though, to warn that this notion of tangency 'is only an ideal limit, never attained in practice.' Of course it *is* attained, at the death of the bull, and sometimes of the *torero*. However, to attain it immediately spells the end of the particular beauty of the bullfight, which is expressed in the pass. The pass indicates a tangency of rule and exception, when it would be death to unite them completely. Still, the passes can become closer, the gap between *torero* and *toro* can narrow more and more, intensifying in the spectators the sense of the sinister, and at the same time of the beautiful. According to Leiris, the aesthetic perception of beauty 'grafts itself in the end on that gap which represents the sinister element under its highest form: obligatory incompleteness, gulf which we seek vainly to fill, breach open to our perdition.'[2]

Plainly Leiris has gone beyond the bullring. He is asserting the presence in every work of art of a gap such as he describes. That gap alone keeps the work from destroying itself. As soon as the exception becomes united with the rule, the transgression with the law, the work's whole shape falls apart. Beauty is swallowed up in death. Yet for a work's beauty to be meaningful, there is a need for it to incorporate as much as possible the exceptions to its rules, the sinister elements that threaten its aesthetic pattern. The gap must be narrowed as much as possible. This naturally involves a certain danger – danger which validates the activity of an author by giving him a heightened sense of writing's reality. For the writer who is concerned with his manhood, this kind of validation may be especially necessary: facing some kind of danger brings his activity more in line with that of the traditional man of action.

In the Afterword to his *Manhood (L'age d'homme)* Leiris begins to develop these ideas in specific relation to autobiography. The *Miroir de la tauromachie* was written between *Manhood* and its Afterword, so it is not surprising that the Afterword is entitled 'The Autobiographer as Torero'. Leiris has moved from 'the terrain of truth', as Spaniards call the bullring, to the terrain of a rather different kind of truth. Yet the same theories seem to hold for both, particularly the need for danger as an innate part of the aesthetic experience:

> Is not what occurs in the domain of style valueless if it remains 'aesthetic,' anodyne, insignificant, if there is nothing in the fact of writing a work that is equivalent . . . to the bull's keen horn, which alone – by reason of the physical danger it represents – affords the *torero*'s art a human reality, prevents it from being no more than the vain grace of a ballerina?
>
> To expose certain obsessions of an emotional or sexual nature, to admit publicly to certain shameful deficiencies or dismays was, for the author, the means – crude, no doubt, but which he entrusts to others, hoping to see it improved – of introducing even the shadow of a bull's horn into a literary work.[3]

This was Leiris's first draft of his ideas. Years later, sitting down to complete the essay, he began to criticize and question the analogy suggested by his younger self – and most of all in regard to the danger faced by the hero-autobiographer. More explicitly now, he linked the bull with the author's own past: 'my life was what it was and I could not alter, by so much as a comma, my past, a primary datum representing for me a fate as unchallengeable as for the *torero* the beast that runs into the ring.'[4] But merely to expose the past may not lead to any danger much more intense than embarrassment. Indeed, told in the right tone, the most sordid revelations become forgivable, even admirable. John Cleland, for instance, recognizes this at the opening of his *Memoirs of a Coxcomb*:

> So delicate is the pleasure, so superior to defending is the

dignity of confessing one's follies, that the wonder is to see so few capable of it. Yet, what does such a confession cost, but the sacrifice of a paltry, miserable, false, self-love, which is forever misleading and betraying us? And of all its illusions there is not perhaps a more silly one, than that which hinders us from discerning that there is scarce a less merit in acknowledging candidly one's faults, than in not having been guilty of them.

Self-love is explicitly condemned here, but only in order that it may be indulged on a less obvious level. Cleland's 'candid' tone is full of delicate ironies that remind us how tone may sometimes cover a multitude of sins, especially sins of self-deception and self-justification. Such a tone, however, is a breach of the fundamental rule to which the writer of confessions is bound: not only must he tell the whole truth and nothing but the truth;

> he must also confront it directly and tell it without artifice, without those great arias intended to make it acceptable, tremolos or catches in the voice, grace notes and gildings which would have no other result than to disguise it to whatever degree, even by merely attenuating its crudity, by making less noticeable what might be shocking about it.[5]

The *torero*, of course, is also bound by rules, which are the whole source of the danger he incurs in that they deliberately place him within reach of the bull's horn. Leiris concludes, 'This fact that the danger incurred depends on a more or less close observation of the rule therefore represents what I can . . . retain of the comparison I chose to establish between my activity as a writer of confessions and that of the *torero*.'[6] This seems clear and conclusive. However, we can learn still more about the kind of danger the autobiographer incurs if we learn more about the rule that binds him, the rule of authenticity.

Authenticity, which seems so at odds with stylization, may sometimes be expressed in terms of a particular style. Leiris resolves 'to speak only of what I knew from experience and what touched me most closely, so that each of my sentences would possess a special density, an affecting plenitude; in other words: the quality proper to what we call "authenticity." '[7] But plenitude is not really a style: it is, in a sense, the very opposite of a style – unattainable by style, and indeed unattainable by writing. Derrida has spoken of our yearning for an impossible dream of plenitude. For Leiris, too, the quality of plenitude in writing is impossible to realize completely. Plenitude always falls short, though it be by an infinitely small margin. Leiris compares this margin to the one drop of water which will always be wanting before the vessel overflows – a drop withheld 'whether because of our fear, a holding back at the last moment; or because of our lucidity itself, which takes the measure of things and introduces this margin of recoil. . . .' The slender margin creates 'an impassable abyss between those two terms: "on this side" and "on the other side." '[8] Certainly in terms of that 'affecting plenitude' Leiris wishes for his words, no words are ever full enough of the authentic experience they claim to render. There is always and inevitably a gap; and it is a gap more poignantly felt to the degree that the style aspires to plenitude. The gap can be narrowed by the rule of authenticity, but it can never be closed completely. The most that can be expected is a kind of tangency, as the artist enfolds the bull of fact closer and closer around his own body. This he does with words, which are as deceptive in their way as the matador's swirling cape. Their deception can evoke truth, coax it towards a union that is ultimately impossible. The gap remains. In autobiography, it has a disconcerting significance: it reveals itself as a gap within one's self. For *torero* and *toro* are only different versions of the same self.

But the gap has another significance specifically related to a writer who, like Leiris, declares his intention to write his manhood.[9] It signifies that which threatens his manhood most: the female in himself. André Masson makes this explicit in his illustrations for the *Miroir de la tauromachie*. One illustration shows the *torero* evading a bull's horn that is patently phallic; and at the tip of the horn, in the space between bull and *torero*, is the 'wound' of the female genitals. In autobiography, as I have just indicated, that wound-like gap is actually a gap within one's self. In trying to close the gap, an autobiographer like Leiris is trying to exorcize his own female element. Like the classic Mexican *macho*, he abhors the idea of an opening in him. Any such gap has female connotations to one whose ideal of manhood is hard invulnerability.

Hardness is a recurrent element in Leiris's private imagery. For a long time he hoped to turn his life into a purely objective work of art; and he described this goal in terms of the solidity and hardness of a statue. In his study of Leiris, Jeffrey Mehlman cites Freud's paper on the petrifaction of spectators by the Medusa's head. He uses it to support his contention that the hardness here is that of the erect penis, and that Leiris's recurrent imagery of self-petrifaction is symptomatic of a desire to be wholly phallic.[10] That desired phallic hardness is inevitably confronted with the gap. It is probably this confrontation which is depicted in a dream that Leiris had in 1928. In this dream, he journeys to the ruined temple of Delphi. Before the temple he finds a great crevasse which 'echoes with a sinister noise', though this is only an effect of the wind and does not portend any seismic disturbance. 'Shortly after this truth has been realized, bearded men – probably officiating priests of the temple – hurl enormous blocks of marble into the abyss. At the bottom, these blocks break into a thousand pieces, making a tremendous racket.'[11] The gap has swallowed up the hard, phallic element, and this seems to be sanctioned by the presence of priests. Leiris's dream heralds a shift in his imagery, and his aesthetic, from self-petrifaction to a gap – a gap which increasingly narrows but always stops short of complete closure, of petrifaction. This shift reflects his new awareness that self-objectivization is a goal that can never be fully attained. A wholly 'phallic' autobiography is not possible; the gap will always be there, and the masculine author will always be attempting to fill it.

To fill a female 'gap' completely is also what is attempted in male sexual activity. And so it is not surprising that Leiris adopts sexual imagery to speak both of bullfighting and of works of art. In bullfighting, the passes have for Leiris a 'to-and-fro rhythm (pressing close and withdrawing alternately, like the movements of coitus).'[12] The French phrasing ('suite de rapprochements et d'éloignements alternés') can be carried over intact to describe the autobiographer's approximations to truth and his distancing from it. For there is also, he says, 'a rhythm – or way in which strong meanings and weak ones are placed end to end – in aesthetic material'.[13] Leiris explicitly links this aesthetic rhythm to the sexual. He is not the only one to have done so. D.H. Lawrence, for instance, writes in the Foreword to *Women in Love*:

In point of style, fault is often found with the continual, slightly modified repetition. The only answer is that it is natural to the author; and that every natural crisis in emotion or passion or understanding comes from this pulsing, frictional to-and-fro, which works up to culmination.[14]

Lawrence's comment makes explicit what is only implicit in Leiris: that repetition will be a characteristic feature of any work that shares these preoccupations and attitudes. The author will pass over the same ground – slightly modifying his approach, perhaps – in an effort to achieve a climax of understanding or emotion or both. His activity is then the equivalent of a bull-fighter's passes, which end in a similarly sexual culmination:

After so many caresses, so increasingly excruciating, the two partners separate, now strangers to each other. It is then that the public ovation explodes and crowns the whole with its release of pleasure. And undoubtedly it would be valid to speak . . . of the ovation as a 'discharge' – a lowering of nervous potential, equal to the break in a fever, and at the same time to an ejaculation. . . .[15]

'Undoubtedly it would be valid,' Leiris claims, but of course the validity of such analogies as this one is not altogether beyond doubt. They are natural enough to him: in *Manhood* Leiris refers to his 'habit of thinking in models, analogies, images – a mental technique of which, whether I like it or not, the present account is only an application.'[16] There are plenty of reasons for him *not* to like this technique. For one thing, analogies, however much they may serve to clarify things, are always more or less fallacious logically. Psychologically, though, analogies are the natural language adopted by the unconscious. They express relations that may seem tenuous only because they are too deeply rooted to be readily perceived. Such relations are incapable of proof by the usual methods. Only an increase in the shared awareness that such relations may exist provides a kind of validation. Leiris's analogy here is shared and even extended by George Steiner, for one:

The interactions of the sexual and the linguistic accompany our whole lives. . . . If coition can be schematized as dialogue, masturbation seems to be correlative with the pulse of monologue or of internalized address. . . . Ejaculation is at once a physiological and a linguistic concept. Semen, excreta, and words are communicative products. They are transmissions from the self inside the skin to reality outside.[17]

When seen as part of this larger analogy, ovation as ejaculation becomes more understandable.

The most significant aspect of Leiris's analogy here is that he situates the climax in the audience. He does this in spite of the bull's death, which could so readily be viewed as sexual. In autobiography, too, the climax is situated in the audience – must necessarily be situated there, for no equivalent to sexual death can exist within the work. In a bullfight, the gap can be closed in death, but only because *toro* is other than *torero*. No such death can occur in autobiography because *torero* and *toro* are the same person. The paradoxes of autobiography do not reach a climax; they do not unite, no matter how narrow the gap between them. There can be, then, no 'moment of truth' in autobiography. There is only the continually shifting terrain of truth. The climax necessarily arises outside that terrain, in the emotion and the understanding of the audience. What the audience understands and feels is something by definition unknowable – unknowable at least in the sense that it cannot be fully articulated and rationalized, by the audience any more than by the author. However, as Merleau-Ponty once observed, we are continually living the solution to problems that reason cannot solve. The understanding has been communicated where it could never be articulated. And in the best of autobiography it is above all an understanding of that gap which is at the heart of self-reflection.

As Leiris, in *Manhood*, analyses his nature through considering remembered images, so I have analysed the images of his Afterword as much for the sake of their psychological content as anything else. It remains to be seen whether that content is valid for Leiris only, or is more widely relevant to autobiographers – in particular, those attempting to write their manhood. The test is to take the theory we have been exploring and apply it to a work by an author other than Leiris. Philip Roth's *My Life as a Man* is, to be sure, a novel; and Leiris has described his autobiographical endeavour as the very 'negation of a novel'.[18] This novel, though, has as its ultimate subject autobiography itself.

My Life as a Man is in two parts. The longer of these is an autobiographical narrative by one Peter Tarnopol, a Jewish American novelist, and it centres around the prolonged agony of his marriage. In the style of movie-magazine confessions, this section is entitled 'My True Story' – an irony in view of Tarnopol's continually articulated difficulties in arriving at any sense of the truth of matters. This section has been preceded by one entitled 'Useful Fictions'. The fictions are two short stories by Peter Tarnopol which draw on the events of his own life and present them through a fictional version of himself named Nathan Zuckerman. Tarnopol is himself a fiction, of course; and as Zuckerman is to Tarnopol, so may Tarnopol be to Roth. We notice certain points of congruency with Philip Roth's own life, but aside from indicating one more layer of complexity to the work that need not concern us here.

'My True Story' is introduced by one of those brief biographies that publishers are so fond of, largely filled with dates and place names. Because this biographical description of Tarnopol is written by Tarnopol himself, though, it is not as arid and neutral as is usually the case. Near the close we are told:

> Presently Mr. Tarnopol is preparing to forsake the art of fiction for a while and embark upon an autobiographical narrative, an endeavor which he approaches warily, uncertain as to both its advisability and usefulness. Not only would the publication of such a personal document raise serious legal and ethical problems, but there is no reason to believe that by keeping his imagination at bay and rigorously adhering to the facts, Mr. Tarnopol will have exorcized his obsession once and for all.[19]

The preoccupations are similar to Leiris's: the rigorous adherence to facts, and also the early recognition of an element of risk, the danger of a 'bull's horn'. As we have seen in Leiris, the danger will go deeper than just 'legal and ethical problems'. Tarnopol's narrative makes increasingly clear that the danger has to do with the difficulty of attaining truth, and most especially about one's self.

Self is the terrain on which Tarnopol fights all his battles. 'His self,' he tells us, 'is to many a novelist what his own physiognomy is to a painter of portraits: the closest subject at hand demanding scrutiny, a problem for his art to solve – given the enormous obstacles to truthfulness, *the* artistic problem.' (p. 240) So he is constantly arguing out his own motives: sometimes with his analyst, Dr Spielvogel; sometimes with the reader; sometimes with himself. At one point Tarnopol considers the possibility of viewing his whole recent output as id, superego, and ego. 'Salad Days', the first of the 'Useful Fictions', is 'something like a comic idyll honoring a Pannish (and as yet unpunished) id'. (p. 113) 'Courting Disaster' is superego by virtue of its heavily responsible and moral tone. And he concludes that the autobiographical narrative might just be the ego, coming forward to have its day in court. His literary activity is then clearly an extension of his 'official' psychoanalysis. It has as justification – in Leiris's words – 'to illuminate certain matters for oneself at the same time as one makes them communicable to others.'[20] All this centering on the self naturally leaves him open to a charge of narcissism; and indeed he tells us that Dr Spielvogel considers him 'among the nation's top young narcissists in the arts'. Tarnopol himself would disagree, claiming that 'the artist's success depends as much as anything on his powers of detachment, on *de*-narcissizing himself.' (p. 240)

The attainment of this sort of detachment does not come easily – for Tarnopol it hardly comes at all. He would like to model himself on Flaubert, but finds it impossible, and considers changing models:

> I'll try a character like Henry Miller, or someone out-and-out bilious like Céline for my hero instead of Gustave Flaubert – and won't be such an Olympian writer as it was my ambition to be back in the days when nothing called personal experience stood between me and aesthetic detachment. (p. 227)

It is for this reason that Tarnopol switches from writing a novel to writing an autobiography: to test 'whether his candor, such as it is, can serve any better than his art'. (p. 101) Such as it is, his candour runs up against another version of the same problem. If Tarnopol cannot purge his art from personal emotions, neither can the recital of his personal emotions be purged from art. The writer persists in subjectively arranging, highlighting, and stylizing an objective experience – indeed, he cannot even truly determine the objective experience, so much is he enmeshed in his own subjectivity. Subjective and objective selves thus circle one another in the familiar pattern of *torero* and *toro*. These selves are at odds, however intimately, and cannot be united. The problems are all implicit in the juxtaposed epigraphs of Karen's imaginary paper (p. 226) on the 'Useful Fictions' of the man who was briefly her professor and even more briefly her lover:

> Certainly I do not deny when I am reading that the author may be impassioned, nor even that he might have conceived the first plan of his work under the sway of passion. But his decision to write supposes that he withdraws somewhat from his feelings . . .
> – Sartre, *What is Literature?*

> On ne peut jamais se connaître, mais seulement se raconter.
> – Simone de Beauvoir

The first epigraph invites us to speculate on precisely how much 'somewhat' is; while the second raises the question of whether, after a certain point, one can really 'recount' oneself without 'knowing' oneself. And if such knowledge is necessarily incomplete, at what stage of incompleteness is the writer justified in declaring himself satisfied? Tarnopol is one of those writers who is never satisfied. The whole of *My Life as a Man* is Tarnopol's attempt, in various ways, to know himself. The book conveys no complete knowledge; it conveys completely the attempt at knowledge.

The attempt is conveyed most of all by a strategy and structuring which is richly self-reflexive. The work incorporates much criticism of itself, which is often challenging or illuminating. On the 'Useful Fictions' we have a paper by Karen, written comments by Tarnopol's sister Joan and two of her literary friends, a brief note from Dr Spielvogel, and another (imaginary) from Tarnopol's dead wife. On the life which is the subject of 'My True Story' we have one version by Dr Spielvogel, a psychoanalytic study published in a scholarly journal; we have another, more damning version by Tarnopol's wife Maureen, articulate everywhere but in the banal pages of her diary; we have minor versions by Tarnopol's brother and sister, and by his lover Susan. But above all we have Tarnopol's own shifting versions of the truth of himself. He passes over the same ground again and again, but never in exactly the same manner. *My Life as a Man* is like the novel Tarnopol is trying to write about his 'misadventures in manhood'; it may even *be* that novel:

> By now the various abandoned drafts had gotten so shuffled together and interwoven . . . that what impressed one upon attempting to penetrate that prose was not the imaginary world it depicted, but the condition of the person who'd been doing the imagining: the manuscript was the message, and the message was Turmoil. (pp. 237–8)

This comment on his novel-in-progress is itself part of a seven-page digression separating the beginning and the end of a single dramatic episode – a common enough occurrence in this book.

No less important than the shifts in subject matter are the shifts in style. Each of the 'Useful Fictions' proposes such a shift in style, which amounts to a fundamental change in attitude. At the end of 'Salad Days', to quote Karen's paper, 'the shield of lightheartedness is all at once pierced by the author's pronouncement that in his estimation the true story really isn't funny at all.' (pp. 226–7) A sequel, the author suggests, 'calls for an approach far more *serious* than that which seems appropriate to the tale of his easeful salad days. To narrate with fidelity the misfortunes of Zuckerman's twenties would require deeper dredging, a darker sense of irony, a grave and pensive voice to replace the amused, Olympian point of view.' (p. 31) 'Courting Disaster' is thus appropriately subtitled 'Serious in the Fifties'. Yet well into this story the author again proposes a shift in style: 'To treat this story as a species of comedy would not require more than a slight alteration in tone and attitude,' he suggests (p. 80), and goes on for a page to explore this idea. What is really being explored, though, is the way in which 'a slight alteration' in attitude can affect an apparently objective reality.

The two stories are *not* objective reality, of course, but 'Useful Fictions'. They are betrayed as such even in the paired versions of Nathan Zuckerman's world, which do not square exactly in their details. Between the two stories, for instance, the father's profession changes from shoe salesman to bookkeeper, the brother becomes a sister, the senior honours paper on Virginia Woolf becomes a projected article on the same subject. Such inconsistencies of detail can have no other purpose than to keep us from too easy a trust in the text's illusion of reality. For that illusion, according to Ortega y Gasset on the novel, is almost entirely dependent on accumulating detail to such a degree that it may compete with the thick texture of details that is the reader's life.[21] The Nathan Zuckerman of 'Courting Disaster' would agree: as a creative writing instructor, he comments, 'It was the accumulation of small details that gave Lydia's stories such distinction as they had.' (p. 63) When we shift from Tarnopol's 'Useful Fictions' to his own 'True Story', the discrepancies become greater, and not just in details. Major events and major characters, though connected to their fictional counterparts, are strikingly different. One wonders most of all about Tarnopol's differences from Zuckerman, and about the degree to which his present recounting of himself may diverge from reality, serving as yet another 'Useful Fiction'. A serious 'credibility gap' has thus opened up, beginning with a few small fissures in the two short stories. The willing suspension of disbelief has itself been suspended. Increasingly in *My Life as a Man* we are made aware of the gap, of the vacancy behind the words.

Of this vacancy Maureen Tarnopol may well be the appropriate Muse. The epigraph to the book, drawn from her diary, indicates this: 'I could be his Muse, if only he'd let me.' But it is important that she is a muse of a particular kind, a kind described by Leiris:

> I am imbued with the notion that a Muse is necessarily a dead woman, inaccessible or absent; that the poetic structure – like a cannon, which is only a hole surrounded by steel – can be based only on what one does not have; and that ultimately one can write only to fill a void or at the very least to situate, in relation to the most lucid part of ourselves, the place where this incommensurable abyss yawns within us.[22]

Though Maureen is in fact dead through much of the narrative, she is still far too present in Tarnopol's life, and is to him the very personification of that gap which can never be closed in his sense of himself. Until it is closed, the author will never feel that he has fully attained the manhood to which he aspires throughout the novel. We are then led once again to the idea of the 'gap' as a female element. As in *Miroir de la tauromachie*, the gap may even be a version of the female sexual organ, just as the writer's

impulse 'to fill a void' may be a projected phallic impulse.
Certainly in Tarnopol's eyes, Maureen is only an extreme
example of the nature of the whole female sex. To him, Maureen
and Susan, otherwise completely dissimilar, are united by a
peculiarly negative quality.

> what drew them together as women – which is to say, what
> drew me to them, for that is the subject here – was that in
> her own extreme and vivid way, each of these antipathetic
> originals demonstrated that sense of defenselessness and
> vulnerability that has come to be a mark of their sex and is often
> at the core of their relations with men. (p. 172)

To call Maureen, especially, 'defenseless' may seem ludicrously
inappropriate, given her power to make Tarnopol's life a hell
on earth. What is being gotten at by this phrasing, though, is a
certain quality of *lack*. In contrast to Tarnopol, who works hard
and is full of his vocation as a writer, both Maureen and Susan
drift aimlessly, with no certain goal in life. Both women use a man
to fill the gap which is themselves, and that man is Tarnopol.
The notion of woman as gap is fundamental to Maureen's role as
Muse of this novel. There are specific ways in which she causes
Tarnopol to fall short of the fulfilment of himself: 'devoting
himself almost exclusively . . . to his nightmarish marriage' (p.
99) causes for Tarnopol an enormous gap in his writing career;
on the marriage front itself 'everything I did was futile, including
of course doing nothing' (p. 167); and finally Maureen consist-
ently shatters any rationale of himself to which Tarnopol might
attain with the cry – actual or imagined – of 'Lies! Filthy, self-
serving lies!' These particular negations of Tarnopol, though, all
spring from the underlying view of Maureen (or women) as gap.
It is a gap with attractions, of course; and I do not mean merely
that both Maureen and Susan are pretty. In 'Courting Disaster' it
is made especially clear that what attracts the narrator to Lydia –
that story's version of Maureen – is precisely the sense of a
terrible gap in her which the narrator wishes to possess and
make his own. For Lydia's sake he throws over a girl who has
everything that a man could possibly desire for his fulfilment –
except that quality which Tarnopol confesses is what drew him
to Maureen and Susan. It draws him aesthetically most of all. For
Tarnopol seems to feel with Leiris that for a work to achieve

greatness full and flawless beauty is not enough. There must also be that sense of the fissure, the gap. And if this holds true in a work of art, it also holds true for the work of art which is Zuckerman's – or Tarnopol's –life.

Naturally enough for a novel whose subject is autobiography, life and literature are intricately related throughout *My Life as a Man*. Early in the book we are told that 'my life was coming to resemble one of those texts upon which certain literary critics of that era used to enjoy venting their ingenuity. I could have done a clever job on it myself for my senior honors thesis in college. . . .' (p. 72) And indeed when the author criticizes his life he often does so in literary terms, as inadequately motivated, or even Not True to Life. Having introduced into his comfortable life that element, in the person of Maureen/Lydia, which his literary sensibilities tell him is required, he finds that it is an element not so easily controlled in life as in literature. He reverses himself: 'Literature got me into this and literature is gonna have to get me out.' (p. 174) If life was seen as literature, literature is now seen, if not as life itself, at least as a way of remaking life. All of Tarnopol's writing is now an effort to clarify his old self and to attain a new one. Given the nature of autobiography, this is an immensely difficult job:

> Tarnopol, as he is called, is beginning to seem as imaginary as my Zuckermans anyway, or at least as detached from the memoirist – his revelations coming to seem like still another 'useful fiction,' and not because I am telling lies. I am trying to keep to the facts. Maybe all I'm saying is that words, being words, only approximate the real thing, and so no matter how close I come, I only come *close*. (p. 231)

As in a good bullfight, the artist may come closer and closer to filling the gap. In the nature of things, though, there can be no 'moment of truth' in autobiography; and so *My Life as a Man* is a book which does not contain a climax. Considering the sexual metaphor underlying Leiris's ideas of both bullfight and autobiography, it is perhaps significant here that neither Maureen nor Susan is ever able to achieve an orgasm – though we are told how Susan comes increasingly close to one. Tarnopol, too, comes increasingly close to filling the gap in his self-knowledge, but can never quite attain it. The book is arranged to dramatize this: incidents occur not chronologically, nor entirely by free-wheeling association, but in increasingly narrow and dangerous versions of the 'gap'. Tarnopol gives himself to us first in the distanced, fictional guise of Nathan Zuckerman, with the second of the two stories – as its subtitle indicates – by far the more serious of the two. When he speaks explicitly of himself in 'My True Story' he does so by stages, in separately titled sections. 'Peppy' merely indicates the dilemma of Tarnopol's marriage and devotes most of its time to his relationship with brother and sister. 'Susan' *actually* followed Maureen chronologically, but precedes her aesthetically as a weaker, more tractable version of the same phenomenon. 'Marriage a la Mode' describes the way in which Maureen tricked Tarnopol into marriage, with considerable assistance from Tarnopol's own literary-aesthetic conscience. We would expect such a section on the marriage itself to be the heart of darkness, but this is by no means the case. The following section, 'Dr. Spielvogel', takes us, through Tarnopol's analyst, deeper into the heart of the author. And here we begin really to sense the 'bull's horn': it is the risk that an increase in knowledge may end by indicting the autobiographer. The section comes very close to doing just that. This is in part because of the new revelations of Tarnopol's conduct: that he had a number of sexual encounters with other women during his marriage, perhaps as purely 'human' as he claims they were; that in a desperate gesture of 'unmanning' himself he once dressed in his wife's bra and panties; that he went through a period of leaving his sperm in public places. In part, too, Tarnopol is indicted by our own growing awareness of his attitude. For instance:

'And what did you do?' asked Spielvogel.
'Did I kick her, you mean? No. No, no, no, no, no.'

Plainly Spielvogel means nothing of the sort. But a minute later:

'And what did you do then?'
'Did I slit her throat from ear to ear? No. No! I fell apart.'
(p. 209)

Of course it is a man under considerable strain who is speaking. But such comments, along with the rhythms of hysteria, and above all the sheer volume of Tarnopol's verbosity combine to create a backlash in the reader. The fellow doth protest too much, we think, and begin to give an emotional credence to the possibility – raised and dismissed several times before – that much of this strain may be of Tarnopol's own making. In the last section, 'Free', we have a final example of this. Against everybody's advice, Tarnopol agrees to a face-to-face meeting with his wife in his own apartment. After a series of taunts and aggravations on the part of his wife, he beats her up severely, indeed 'pretending' at one point that he is going to murder her. For this episode Susan's comments are most apt: 'The woman is a psychopath, you tell me that yourself. What is gained by beating up someone who isn't even responsible for what she says?' But her comments on Tarnopol are even more apt:

> You keep trying to do the 'manly' thing, and all you ever do is act like a child. . . . There *is* no 'manly' thing with her. Don't you see that yet? There are only crazy things. Crazier and crazier! But you're like a little boy in a Superman suit, with some little boy's ideas about being big and strong. Every time she throws down the glove, *you* pick it up!

Her conclusion about the whole 'trap' that Tarnopol feels he is in is that 'the trap is *you*. You're the trap.' (pp. 290–1) And this is perhaps as close as the bull's horn comes in the whole book. To add much more in the way of indictments would be to break the surface tension of the work entirely – would be, in Leiris's image, for the vessel to overflow, and for us to find ourselves not on 'this side' – the narrator's side – but on 'the other side'. A few pages after this point Maureen is killed suddenly in a car crash, and the situation is ended without, really, ever being concluded. As Dr Spielvogel puts it, 'You have been released.'

> 'Free,' I said.
> 'That I don't know about,' said Spielvogel, 'but certainly released.' (p. 327)

It is not so much Maureen's sudden and violent death as it is this sudden and terrifying release that casts its shadow over the book's last pages. Maureen, the very personification of a sinister gap in Tarnopol's life, has been removed. If the gap remains, it must be within himself. It is perhaps the unconscious realization of this possibility that accounts for Tarnopol's state of mind in the book's final paragraph:

> Then, eyes leaking, teeth chattering, not at all the picture of a man whose nemesis has ceased to exist and who once again is his own lord and master, I turned to Susan, still sitting there huddled up in her coat, looking, to my abashment, as helpless as the day I had found her. Sitting there *waiting*. Oh, my God, I thought – now you. You being you! And me! This me who is me being me and none other!

The 'feminine' weakness of Tarnopol's behaviour here is contrasted with a masculine ideal of mastery. A preoccupation with the masculine is made explicit not only in the title of *My Life as a Man* but in references throughout the book. The 'Useful Fictions' close with the author's regretful realization that he has 'squandered my manhood'. Susan's analysis of Tarnopol's fixation on the 'manly' thing squares with his own express desires: 'How do I ever get to be what is described in the literature as *a man?*' (p. 299) And again: 'I wanted to be humanish: manly, a man.' (p. 173) That it is a particularly masculine version of the 'humanish' that Tarnopol aspires to is made clear by the details of his behaviour: for instance, that he will intersperse his meditations with an examination of his penis. This overriding aspiration to the fulfilment of his masculinity informs Tarnopol's literary endeavours, too – making of them all, as with Leiris, an attempt to write his own manhood. We have seen how this involves the drive towards a certain self with a certain kind of knowledge. The whole form and aesthetic of *My Life as a Man* – and not just a collection of scattered references to manhood – expresses this fundamental drive.

But if we are to maintain that this drive, this form, this perception even, is particularly male we should compare it with a female counterpart, and one which as nearly as possible shares the same concerns. Such a female counterpart is Doris Lessing's *The Golden Notebook*. Largely by virtue of the prominence assigned to a sexual consciousness, *The Golden Notebook* has for a long time been read as if its subtitle were *My Life as a Woman*. Anticipating, in 1962, the rise of the Women's Liberation Movement, it took as its subject a woman struggling to lead her own life, free from any false stereotyping. It powerfully expressed the texture of such a woman's daily existence and the currents of her thought and feeling. It showed her coming to a crisis of self-knowledge which is as much as anything else a new knowledge of herself *as* a woman. Further similarities to *My Life as a Man* are evident. *The Golden Notebook* is about Anna Wulf, a writer whose life has many points of congruency with Lessing's own. Anna is a writer with a block, like Tarnopol; and like Tarnopol she is in analysis. *The Golden Notebook* is about Anna Wulf's self-discovery and the relation of her writing to that self-discovery. It assembles many kinds of writing by Anna. We have *Free Women*, the short novel that Anna finally writes – a fictional version of her own life with the distancing and the discrepancies of detail that such a fictionalizing implies. But the most important characteristic of *Free Women* is its flatness, its inadequacy to convey the complex reality of Anna's existence, as we learn of it through her journals. This is a deliberate strategy on Lessing's part, and is emphasized by setting *Free Women* in a different type face from the rest of the book, printing its title in flowery capitals, and making use of rather Victorian chapter descriptions (e.g., 'Two Visits, some telephone calls and a Tragedy'). Interspersed with this novel, we have four notebooks, each dealing with a different aspect of Anna's self. The black notebook gives us a parodic synopsis of her one successful novel, and then explores in depth the memories of Africa from which that novel was drawn. The yellow notebook is an incomplete novel, *The Shadow of the Third*, about Ella, a novelist who has a five-year relationship with a married man – an episode essentially from Anna's own life. The red notebook is about her political life with the communist party. The blue notebook is an attempt at keeping a completely objective diary. All of these notebooks are abandoned as the divisions within Anna's self come down in the final act of self-knowledge. A new notebook, the golden notebook, records Anna's experience of giving herself to madness at a time during which she allows herself to explore everything that has been left out of her identity. Here Anna Wulf differs from Tarnopol, who wishes to confront the negations of his identity only as antagonists, to be overcome in order to close the gap in himself.

The major difference between the two books is in their attitude to the 'gap' in all its layers of meaning: as sexual organ, as gap in self-knowledge, as an inadequacy of words. The aim of *The Golden Notebook* is not, as in *My Life as a Man*, to come closer and closer with words to some unattainable moment of truth. Rather it is to make 'a wordless statement',[23] Lessing tells us. The shape of Roth's novel reflects his aim, in ways we have already seen. In contrast, Lessing's novel derives its shape from a nonverbal construct, the Jungian mandala. Whereas Tarnopol's analyst is a Freudian, Anna Wulf's analyst is a Jungian; and if she were given to literary analysis, she could undoubtedly point out to Anna that her four coloured notebooks correspond to the principle of quaternity which underlies every mandala, however complex. The colour of the golden notebook itself is commonly that of the centre portion which unites all separate manifestations of the self; it is the very heart of the blossom. The attempts to objectify the self by means of various arrangements all take their substance and energy from that subjective centre, itself unknowable. As the unknowable aspect of self, that golden centre corresponds to the 'gap' which I have spoken of at such great length before. Except that the attitude toward that unknowable element, that negation of all conscious identities, is now so different that the term 'gap' is wholly inappropriate. If a new term had to be found for something by definition indescribable, perhaps the idea of 'inner space' might do.[24] Such an inner space is not something to be closed, nor to be flirted with as with a great danger. Rather it is the sacred and unknowable source of self. All else – the words and actions which make up what we choose to call our identities – is a momentary and incomplete manifestation of its power. If this is a woman's view more often than it is a man's (and we can never have conclusive evidence on the matter) it may be because her perceptions are influenced by the physical metaphor of her own body; or it may be because men have been conditioned to believe that power and control are their natural rights as men, not only over others but over their most intimate selves.

Leiris, in the years that follow the writing of *Manhood*, is able to waive the male privilege that Tarnopol aspires to, that of being his own lord and master. He learns to incorporate the gap within him, but not before he has pursued his old aspirations to stony self-objectification, even to the extreme of death. In *Manhood* Leiris ultimately argues that the only possibility of closing the gap, of achieving full communion with oneself, lies in suicide.

Through suicide, he says, one attains the resolution of all paradoxes: one becomes 'at the same time *oneself and the other*, male
and female, subject and object, killed and killer'.[25] Leiris's suicide
attempt – an insufficient dose of poison – succeeds only as
gesture, allowing him to exclaim, just before dropping unconscious in front of his wife, 'Tout ça, c'est la littérature.' He
emerges from the hospital recovered not only from his suicide
attempt but also from the literary aspiration towards phallic
plenitude. To save him from the poison it has been necessary to
perform a tracheotomy, and Leiris now bears on his throat its
scar: sign of the gap which he has incorporated into his own
body and, metaphorically, into his voice.

That gap is one which is at the heart of all writing and at the
heart of all human selves. Yet the gap is given a sex – without any
real warrant for this other than a biological parallel to what itself
is just a metaphor. It is felt to be female; and the male aspires to
close it, while knowing perfectly well that this is impossible to
attain. Only death closes the gap and consummates manhood.
Once more, then, we have the intimate relationship between
masculinity and death. In an extreme case like Mishima's, death
has been the validation of his role as a man; it has played its part
in the specific masculine roles that have been considered here; it
has, at the least, provided the thrill of danger so necessary to
make an experience 'masculine'. Leiris's understanding of manhood has been much like that of all the men in this book who have
attempted, like him, to write their own manhood. Within such
an understanding it is impossible to attain that goal. Fully to
write one's manhood would be to write one's death.

AFTERWORD

For a number of reasons, it is necessary to say more. One reason is that I have no desire to end this book with death as its closing chord. That implies an unwarranted pessimism, when there is every reason for optimism about masculinity at this point in time, with its tremendous release of new forms of energy and awareness. Awareness of any sort is constructive, even if it be of a destructive pattern. In this case the face of death has been revealed as the other side of a coin, the common currency of manhood. The masculine ideal of strength and complete control is joined to its opposite by the closest of all possible relations between opposites – that of paradox. Again and again in works by the School of Virility the very drive for control is itself the cause of control's dissolution. The men who pursue this control have their own kind of vital energy; ultimately, though, they lose the deeper *élan vital*, that flexible principle which includes all possibilities and not just that of manhood. This may account for the nihilism and sense of loss underlying many of the works dealt with here, even (or especially) those which intend to celebrate the traditional masculine stance.

Such a dubious sense of things is echoed outside of literature by the men most conscious of changes in their role: the members of the still-fumbling Men's Movement. If the movement has not yet 'caught on' to the same degree as the Women's Movement, this is not because it is any the less needed. It is mainly that both movements have reversed the popular understanding of a sex role, and in the case of the masculine role, the reversal has not seemed a very affirmative one. Many men have swung from one extreme of power and self-congratulation to another extreme of despair and self-denigration. Similarly, many women swung from an extreme of compliant docility to an opposite extreme of rage. These extremes are necessary in any process of growth. William Blake, for one, would approve: 'Without Contraries there is no Progression.' Yet there is always the danger that one may stick at one extreme or another. After centuries during which a sex role has been affirmed in terms of one extreme, it is not surprising that individuals may spend their lives obsessively affirming the opposite. And they pay the price that one always pays for affirming only one extreme: they become grotesques. In 'The Book of the Grotesque' that opens *Winesburg, Ohio,* Sherwood Anderson tells a kind of fable about the varied and opposed truths in the world, all of which are beautiful. Then the people appear; and 'the moment one of the people took one of the truths to himself, called it his truth, and tried to live his life by it, he became a grotesque and the truth he embraced became a falsehood.' Mishima is one example, in his explicit disregard of all other truths but the one he chose to pursue. In fact all of the writers dealt with in this book partake of this quality, in so far as they are a group of deliberately selected extreme cases. A part of their humanity tyrannizes over the whole. They are led by their penises, in some cases to death.

Self-destructiveness is one aspect of the self-consciousness that is a defining characteristic of men in this century. That 'virility has now become self-conscious', as Virginia Woolf declares, means that it has turned in upon itself. The self-conscious person thinks first about self; and then, since the self is a thinking self, he thinks about thinking. Soon he is caught in a reflexive phenomenon like that of two mirrors placed face to face. Such an infinite regression inevitably paralyses a simpler kind of progression. Action, which is so central to the traditional idea of manhood, becomes 'sicklied o'er with the pale cast of thought'; the he-man becomes Hamlet. He is perfectly capable of acting, it's true, but without the same spontaneity and confidence in his natural virility. As the moments of 'natural' virility elude a man over and over again, he begins to shore up his sense of manhood with theory, with language, with artifice. He begins, perhaps, to 'protest too much'. His manly actions have become a style.

A style is capable both of petrifying a self and of calling a new self into being. The writers dealt with in this book fall somewhere between these alternatives. These men are far from simply accepting the traditional role; they are aware, much more than is the common garden-variety *macho*, of that role's complexities and paradoxes. Yet they will not free themselves of the role's hold over them. Instead, they circle around it, in simultaneous attraction and repulsion, centripetal and centrifugal force. Their writing styles, even in the most 'masculine' versions, reflect this ambivalence. In comparison, we may recall Virginia Woolf's ideas on the use of a particularly 'female' writing style. The style of the 'new woman' is so suited to the female mind that its author can forget about being a woman. Without a crippling self-consciousness of sex, the author simply writes; and that which is innately female in her is free to emerge naturally. Nothing so easy as this seems to be going on now for either male or female writers. Eventually, perhaps, both a 'new woman' and a 'new man' will evolve; and their newness will be at the same time the most natural thing in the world. Generations to come will wonder what all the fuss was about, all this laying of individuals on the Procrustean bed of sex roles. That, however, will happen at a time when this type of self-consciousness has succeeded in annihilating itself, and even the sense of the annihilation process. For now, it is a good thing for self-consciousness to nibble away at assumptions about the sexes, all too often unconsciously adopted. Literary criticism of existing styles is one way of calling such assumptions into consciousness, and that has been a major purpose of this book.

Such a purpose cannot be fulfilled by any one book. So another reason to say more in this Afterword is to claim less for what I am saying. When speaking of men and women, it is easy to become pontifical. And it is easy for one's statements to be given a more rigid authority or wider application than they will bear. If distrust of authority is typical of today's writers, as Ellman claims, then I am a creature of my time – especially when the authority is me. Dropping the impersonal mask of authority, I must then speak about myself. Feminist critics before me have reintroduced the first person singular into literary criticism. They are not doing so out of egoism, but out of a sense that all we really know is our own experience; and this should be admitted when speaking of any experience so intimate as the sense of one's own sex. I have tried, in these chapters, to be something of a chameleon – to take on the colouring of the works in order to read them on their own terms. Yet the particular slant taken here has to be my own. The self-consciousness that plays so important a role here is certainly my own. Some men I have talked to do not share it; and I don't feel that they are in need of self-consciousness-raising. I only know that their experience of the male role is rather different from mine, just as I know that many other men's experiences are similar.

Similarities and differences must be held in the head simultaneously, resisting the temptation to exaggerate in either direction. This applies to men as a group; to men and women; to the individual and the whole of humanity. My own preference is for differences, because they preserve the individual. This has made me somewhat reluctant throughout the book to state my general conclusions about men. Such conclusions close off. Like any sexual style itself, they inhibit the sense of individual differences. Consequently, I have shied away from defining manhood in either an old or a new version. At the same time, it has been the underlying impetus of the whole book, if not to define manhood, at least to explore it so that the reader may be more conscious of its nature. Perhaps that is what is really meant by a 'raised consciousness'. With it, the reader may create definitions that are useful at the time; may melt those down and forge new definitions; and so on in a process as long as life. In this way we may ultimately reach an understanding that is without definition, wordless.

NOTES

Introduction

1 Rosalind Miles, *The Fiction of Sex* (New York: Barnes & Noble, 1974), 10.

2 Patricia Meyer Spacks, *The Female Imagination* (New York: Knopf, 1975), 19.

3 Kate Millett, *Sexual Politics* (New York: Doubleday, 1970), 215.

4 Gillian Avery, *Childhood's Pattern* (London: Hodder & Stoughton, 1975), 183.

5 Norman Mailer, *The Prisoner of Sex* (Boston: Little, Brown & Co., 1971), 39–40.

6 Virginia Woolf, *Contemporary Writers* (New York: Harcourt, Brace & World, 1966), 124–5.

7 Dorothy Richardson, *Pilgrimage* (London: J.M. Dent, 1938), IV, 153.

8 Virginia Woolf, *To the Lighthouse* (New York: Harcourt, Brace & Co., 1927), 99–100.

9 Josephine Donovan, 'Feminist Style Criticism' in Susan Koppelman Cornillon, ed., *Images of Women in Fiction* (Bowling Green: Bowling Green University Popular Press, 1973), 344–6.

10 Miles, 53. But note Charles Dickens's letter to Eliot (July 10, 1859) in which he speaks of 'the faith that was in me that you were a woman.'

11 Virginia Woolf, *A Room of One's Own* (New York: Harcourt, Brace, 1929), 133.

12 Mary Ellmann, *Thinking About Women* (New York: Harcourt, Brace, Jovanovich, 1968), 150.

13 Ellmann, 167.

14 Annette Kolodny, 'Some Notes on Defining a "Feminist Literary Criticism",' *Critical Inquiry* 2 (Autumn 1975), 78.

15 There are more books on this subject than can comfortably be cited here. Some of the more noteworthy are: Warren Farrell, *The Liberated Man* (New York: Random House, 1974); *The Forty-nine Percent Majority*, ed. Deborah S. David and Robert Brannon (Reading, Mass.: Addision-Wesley, 1976); Phyllis Chesler, *About Men* (New York: Simon & Schuster, 1978); Leonard Kriegel, *Of Men and Manhood* (New York: Dutton, 1979); and Joseph Pleck, *The Myth of Masculinity*

(Cambridge, Mass.: M.I.T. Press, 1981). The current interest in masculinity has shown up in such scholarly books as Charles J. Haberstroh, Jr., *Melville and Male Identity* (Cranbury, N. J.: Associated University Presses, 1980) and Coppelia Kahn, *Man's Estate: Masculinity and Shakespeare* (Berkeley: University of California Press, 1981).

16 Emerson, *English Traits* (Cambridge, Mass.: Harvard U. Press, 1966), 152–3. Otto Jesperson, in *Growth and Structure of the English Language* (Leipzig: B. G. Teubner, 1905), makes a more systematic attempt to support his contention that the English language is 'positively and expressly masculine'. He cites as masculine characteristics its well-defined consonants, its economy, its numerous monosyllabic words, its moderate intonations, its tendency to understatement.

17 Walter Pater, 'Plato's Esthetics' in *Plato and Platonism* (New York: 1899), 253. Cited in Ellmann.

18 *The Correspondence of Gerard Manley Hopkins and Richard Watson Dixon*, ed. C. G. Abbott (London: Oxford University Press, 1935), 133. Cited by Sandra M. Gilbert and Susan Gubar in *The Madwoman in the Attic* (New Haven: Yale University Press, 1979).

19 Woolf, *A Room of One's Own*, 176.

20 A full examination of the historical circumstances that underlie this shift is beyond my scope here. The interested reader should see Joe L. Dubbert, *A Man's Place: Masculinity in Transition* (Englewood Cliffs, N.J.: Prentice-Hall, 1979) and Peter G. Filene, *Him/Her Self: Sex Roles in Modern America* (New York: Harcourt Brace Jovanovich, 1975), especially pp. 77 ff.

21 Nancy Henley and Barrie Thorne, *Language and Sex: Difference and Dominance* (Rowley, Mass.: Newbury House, 1975), 18.

22 Woolf, *A Room of One's Own*, 108.

23 Georg Simmel, quoted by Viola Klein in *Feminine Character: A Study of Ideology* (London: Routledge, 1946), 82.

24 Woolf, *A Room of One's Own*, 161–2.

25 Woolf, *A Room of One's Own*, 132.

26 Dorothy Richardson, *Pilgrimage* I, 10.

27 James Tiptree, Jr., *Warm Worlds and Otherwise* (New York: Del Ray, 1975), xii, xviii.

28 Shulamith Firestone, *The Dialectic of Sex* (New York: Morrow, 1970), 182.

29 Yukio Mishima, *Sun and Steel*, John Bester (New York: Grove Press, 1970), 47.

1 The language of men

1 Norman Mailer, *Advertisements for Myself* (New York: Putnam, 1959), 472.

2 Warren Farrell, *The Liberated Man* (New York: Bantam, 1975), 62.

3 Norman Mailer, *Cannibals and Christians* (New York: Dial Press, 1966), 201.

4 Mailer, *Advertisements for Myself*, 222.
5 Norman Mailer, *The Armies of the Night* (New York: New American Library, 1968), 25.
6 Norman Mailer, *The Prisoner of Sex* (Boston: Little, Brown & Co., 1971), 168.
7 Mailer, *The Prisoner of Sex*, 132.
8 Mailer, *The Prisoner of Sex*, 9.
9 Mailer, *Cannibals and Christians*, 104–7.
10 Richard Poirier, *Norman Mailer* (New York: Viking Press, 1972), 107.
11 Mary Ritchie Key, *Male/Female Language* (Metuchen, N.J.: Scarecrow Press, 1975), 104.
12 Sandra M. Gilbert and Susan Gubar, *The Madwoman in the Attic* (New Haven: Yale University Press, 1979), xi, 51.
13 Hélène Cixous, 'The Laugh of the Medusa', *Signs* I, no. 4 (Summer 1976), 875–93.
14 See Colin Murray Turbayne, *The Myth of Metaphor*, revised ed. (Columbia: U. of South Carolina Press, 1970).
15 Mailer, *Advertisements for Myself*, p. 17.
16 Nancy Henley and Barrie Thorne, *Language and Sex: Difference and Dominance* (Rowley, Mass.: Newbury House, 1975), 15. As Cheris Kramer observes later in this book, though, 'Beliefs about sex-related differences may be as important as actual differences' (p. 233).
17 Otto Jesperson, *Language* (New York: Henry Holt, 1921), 252.
18 Henley and Thorne, 82, 263–4.
19 Norman Mailer, *The Executioner's Song* (Boston: Little, Brown, 1979), 858.
20 The comparison is Hemingway's own as reported by Lillian Ross in *The New Yorker*, 13 May, 1950.
21 George Steiner, *After Babel: Aspects of Language and Translation* (New York & London: Oxford University Press, 1975), 41.
22 Robin Lakoff, *Language and Woman's Place* (New York: Octagon, 1976), 59.
23 Lakoff, 8.
24 *Henry Miller on Writing* (New York: New Directions, 1964), 186–7.
25 H. Wentworth and S. Flexner, eds, *Dictionary of American Slang* (New York: Thomas Y. Crowell, 1960), xii.
26 Jean Genet, *Our Lady of the Flowers*, trans. Bernard Frechtman (New York: Grove Press, 1963), 90.
27 Jesperson, 246.
28 Henley and Thorne, 45.
29 Henley and Thorne, 45.
30 John Stuart Blackie, tr., *The Lyrical Dramas of Aeschylus* (London: J. M. Dent, 1906), 6.
31 Mailer, *Advertisements for Myself*, 236.
32 Mailer, *Cannibals and Christians*, 90.
33 Robert F. Lucid, ed., *Norman Mailer: The Man and His Work* (Boston: Little, Brown, 1971), 88.
34 Mailer, *Existential Errands* (Boston: Little, Brown & Co., 1963), 119–20.

Compare this last pronouncement to the episode of Ruta's 'Verboten!' and Rojack's 'creative' sex in *An American Dream*.
35 Mailer, *Advertisements for Myself*, 265.
36 Norman Mailer, *Genius and Lust* (New York: Grove Press, 1976), 431.
37 Norman Mailer, *Barbary Shore* (London: Jonathan Cape, 1952), 10.
38 Norman Mailer, *An American Dream* (New York: Dial, 1968), 46.
39 Mailer, *Cannibals and Christians*, 24.
40 Norman Mailer, *The Presidential Papers* (New York: Putnam, 1963), 11.
41 Quoted in Brock Brower, 'Always the Challenger', *Life*, 24 September 1965, 102.
42 Judith Fetterley, *The Resisting Reader* (Bloomington: Indiana University Press, 1978), 160.
43 Mailer, *Advertisements for Myself*, 184.
44 Mailer, *Advertisements for Myself*, 237.
45 Mailer, *The Prisoner of Sex*, 44–5.
46 Fetterley, 155.
47 Mailer, *Cannibals and Christians*, 119.
48 Josephine Donovan, 'Feminist Style Criticism' in Susan Koppelman Cornillon, ed., *Images of Women in Fiction* (Bowling Green: Bowling Green University Popular Press, 1973). And see Helen Deutsch in Lisa Appignanesi, *Femininity and the Creative Imagination* (New York: Barnes & Noble, 1973), 8.
49 Mailer, *Cannibals and Christians*, 113.
50 Mailer, *Cannibals and Christians*, 112.
51 Mailer, *Advertisements for Myself*, 18.

2 Reserve and its reverse

1 Norman Mailer, *Advertisements for Myself* (New York: Putnam, 1959), 19.
2 'Bull in the Afternoon', reprinted in *Ernest Hemingway: The Man and His Work*, John K.M. McCaffery, ed. (New York: Cooper Square Publishers, 1969).
3 Mark Schorer, 'The Background of a Style', *Kenyon Review* 3 (1941), 103.
4 Constance Cappel Montgomery, *Hemingway in Michigan* (New York: Fleet, 1966), 55. Sheridan Baker concurs in this opinion.
5 Sheridan Baker, *Ernest Hemingway: an introduction and interpretation* (New York: Holt, Rinehart & Winston, 1967), p. 4.
6 Sheldon Norman Grebstein, *Hemingway's Craft* (Carbondale, Southern Illinois University Press, 1973), 136.
7 Scott Donaldson, *By Force of Will: The Life and Art of Ernest Hemingway* (New York: Viking Press, 1977), 246.
8 Charles Fenton, *The Apprenticeship of Ernest Hemingway: The Early Years* (New York: Viking Press, 1958), 229–36.
9 *Hemingway and His Critics*, ed. Carlos Baker (New York: Hill & Wong, 1961), 60.
10 Ernest Hemingway, *A Moveable Feast* (New York: Scribner, 1964), 75.

11 Ernest Hemingway, *The Nick Adams Stories* (New York: Scribner, 1972), 19.
12 Octavio Paz, *The Labyrinth of Solitude: life and thought in Mexico*, trans. Lysander Kemp (New York: Grove Press, 1962), 22–3.
13 Hemingway, *A Moveable Feast*, p. 76.
14 Jacques Derrida, *Of Grammatology*, trans. Gayatri Chakravorty Spivak (Baltimore: Johns Hopkins University Press, 1976), xxxvi.
15 Derrida, xxxvii.

3 The cult of the body

1 John Nathan, *Mishima: A Biography* (Boston: Little, Brown, 1974), 13–14.
2 Mishima, *Runaway Horses* (New York: Knopf, 1973), 344.
3 Mishima, *Sun and Steel* (Tokyo: Kodansha International, 1970), 57.
4 Mishima, *Sun and Steel*, 6.
5 Mishima, *Sun and Steel*, 64.
6 Mishima, *The Decay of the Angel* (New York: Knopf, 1974), 68.
7 Mishima, *The Decay of the Angel*, 15.
8 Mishima, *The Decay of the Angel*, 13–14.
9 Mishima, *The Decay of the Angel*, 76.
10 Mishima, *The Temple of Dawn* (New York: Knopf, 1973), 277.
11 Mishima, *The Decay of the Angel*, 146.
12 Mishima, *The Temple of Dawn*, 182.
13 Mishima, *Sun and Steel*, 10–11.
14 Mishima, *Decay of the Angel*, 76. This is the boxer's philosophy in *Kyoko's House*, as yet untranslated. See Nathan, 162.
15 Mishima, *Confessions of a Mask* (Norfolk, Conn.: New Directions, 1958), 63.
16 Mishima, *Sun and Steel*, 15.
17 Mishima, *Sun and Steel*, 53.
18 Mishima, *Sun and Steel*, 15.
19 Nathan, 167.
20 Mishima, *Sun and Steel*, 9.
21 Mishima, *Sun and Steel*, 35.
22 Mishima, *Sun and Steel*, 63.
23 Mishima, *Sun and Steel*, 64–5.
24 Mishima, *Sun and Steel*, 10.
25 Mishima, *Sun and Steel*, 27.
26 Mishima, *Sun and Steel*, 78–9.
27 Mishima, *Sun and Steel*, 46.
28 Mishima, *Sun and Steel*, 44.
29 Mishima, *Sun and Steel*, 45.
30 Mishima, *Sun and Steel*, 44–5.
31 Mishima, *Sun and Steel*, 16.
32 Mishima, *Sun and Steel*, 29.
33 Mishima, *Sun and Steel*, 82.

34 Mishima, *Sun and Steel*, 81–2.
35 Mishima, *Sun and Steel*, 66–7.
36 Mishima, *The Temple of Dawn*, 119.
37 Mishima, *The Decay of the Angel*, 88.
38 Nathan, 269.
39 Mishima, *The Temple of Dawn*, 10.
40 Mishima, *Sun and Steel*, 48–9.
41 Nathan, 269.

4 The pen and the penis

1 Margaret Walters, *The Nude Male: A New Perspective* (New York: Penguin, 1979).
2 *Rolling Stone*, 9 October 1975. See also Angela Carter, 'A Well-hung Hang-up' in *Arts in Society*, ed. Paul Barker (Glasgow: Fontana, 1977).
3 Cited in Mark Strage, *The Durable Fig Leaf* (New York: William Morrow, 1980), 124.
4 D. H. Lawrence, *John Thomas and Lady Jane* (New York: Viking, 1972), 232–3.
5 Phillip Roth, *Portnoy's Complaint* (New York: Random House, 1969), 257.
6 Alberto Moravia, *The Two of Us* (London: Secker & Warburg, 1972), 222.
7 Moravia, 111.
8 Moravia, 351.
9 'It was the phallus, and not any image derived from the female body, which came to represent fertility, and the creative and renewing powers of nature,' says Margaret Walters in *The Nude Male*. This is dramatically rendered by Rico's dream in *The Two of Us* (p. 226). See also Richard Payne Knight and Thomas Wright, *Sexual Symbolism: A History of Phallic Worship* (New York: Julian Press, 1957).
10 Claes Oldenburg, *Store Days* (New York: Something Else Press, 1967), 39.
11 *Death in the Afternoon* (London: Jonathan Cape, 1932), 56.
12 *New York Times Book Review*, 24 October 1976, 2.
13 Mikhail Bakhtin, *Rabelais and his World* (Cambridge, Mass.: M.I.T. Press, 1968), 317.
14 *The Grotesque in Art and Literature* (Gloucester, Mass.: Peter Smith, 1968), 184.
15 *The Grotesque* (London: Methuen, 1972), 27.
16 This is the last illustration in Margaret Walters, *The Nude Male*.

5 The novel as a dirty joke

1 Robert Kroetsch, *Badlands* (Toronto: New Press, 1975), 2. References to this edition will be given within the text in parentheses.

2 Robert Kroetsch, *The Studhorse Man* (London: Macdonald, 1969), 146. References to this edition are given within the text in parentheses.
3 Kroetsch, *Badlands*, 45.
4 Geoff Hancock, 'Interview with Robert Kroetsch', *Canadian Fiction Magazine*, 24–5: 39.
5 Donald Cameron, *Conversations with Canadian Novelists* (Toronto: Macmillan, 1973), 84.
6 Gershon Legman, *Rationale of the Dirty Joke: An Analysis of Sexual Humor*, Second Series (New York: Breaking Point, 1975), 29.
7 Legman, 16.
8 Sigmund Freud, *Wit and its Relation to the Unconscious* (London: Kegan Paul, 1922), 226, 234. There are objections that could be raised to Freud's theories here, and one of them is that the telling of dirty jokes is commonly a masculine ritual. Yet men are supposed to have far fewer inhibitions about sex than women do, particularly in Freud's day. With so many sexual inhibitions to release, women should by rights be coming out with perfectly orgasmic guffaws. I don't think, though, that the notion of a woman laughing at a dirty joke had ever occurred to Freud. This is because he sees the dirty joke as essentially anti-female:

> The smutty joke was originally directed against the woman and is comparable to an attempt at seduction. If a man tells or listens to obscene jokes in male society, the original situation, which cannot be realized on account of sexual inhibitions, is thereby also represented. Whoever laughs at a dirty joke does the same as a spectator who laughs at a sexual aggression. (*Wit*, 140)

If the dirty joke is thus a form of verbal rape, it is no wonder that Freud cannot conceive of a woman laughing at one. The trouble with this is that everyone now knows of women who will laugh uproariously at a dirty joke – and not necessarily the kind of woman who would aid and abet male aggression. Perhaps the theory needs to be more flexible, since laughter is often a matter of the circumstances of the telling and the nature of the particular dirty joke. In an all-male context, Freud's contention that any dirty joke is an aggression against the woman is probably valid. Even when males make their own sexuality the target of the joke – in the one about the corpse with the large whang, for instance – there is a submerged hostility. Though no woman appears in the joke, woman is always, by implication, the audience and judge of a man's sexuality. In a common twist, women are therefore 'to blame' for a man's incapacity – as evidenced by the fact that most rapists are not 'studs' unable to contain themselves, but sexual failures seeking revenge. This same joke told by a woman to other women might have a very different effect.

The whole effect of audience and context on the experience of a dirty joke has not really been investigated enough – certainly not by Freud. Legman has made some interesting suggestions about the relation between teller and listener, but they are not pursued to any great degree.

9 Interview with Russell M. Brown in *The University of Windsor Review* VII, 2 (Spring, 1972), 11.
10 Robert Kroetsch, *The Crow Journals*, 25.
11 Cameron, 89.
12 Kroetsch, *The Crow Journals*, 19.
13 Brown interview, 9.

6 A fabled hunting

1 James Dickey, *Deliverance* (Boston: Houghton Mifflin, 1970); Norman Mailer, *Why Are We in Vietnam?* (London: Weidenfeld & Nicolson, 1969); Robert F. Jones, *Blood Sport* (New York: Dell, 1974). References to these editions will be given within the text in parentheses.
2 See Linda Tarte Holley, 'Design and Focus in James Dickey's *Deliverance*', *South Carolina Review* 10, iii, 90–8.
3 Jose Ortega y Gasset, *Meditations on Hunting* (New York: Charles Scribner, 1972), 59.
4 In *A Man's Place*, the historian Joe Dubbert finds this nostalgia to be a recurrent characteristic of American masculinity; Mishima pays tribute to it in the opening pages of his tetralogy; and in *A Fan's Notes* it explains Frederick Exley's devotion to the game:
> Why did football bring me so to life? I can't say precisely. Part of it was my feeling that football was an island of directness in a world of circumspection. In football a man was asked to do a difficult and brutal job, and he either did it or got out. There was nothing rhetorical or vague about it; I chose to believe it was not unlike the jobs which all men, in some sunnier past, had been called upon to do. It smacked of something old, something unclouded by legerdemain and subterfuge. (p. 8)
5 Fredric Jameson, 'The Great American Hunter, or, Ideological Content in the Novel', *College English* 34 (1972), 183.
6 Joseph Campbell, *The Hero With a Thousand Faces* (Princeton, N.J.: Princeton University Press, 1968), 30.
7 James Dickey, *Sorties* (New York: Doubleday, 1971), 59.
8 Rosemary Jackson, *Fantasy: The Literature of Subversion* (London: Methuen, 1981), 3. I am obviously making my own use of Jackson's comments on fantasy, a use which does not in all respects conform to hers – or to those of Todorov, on whom she bases her ideas. *Deliverance* is admittedly not a fantasy in the literary sense of the word. *Blood Sport*, on the other hand, is; and to emphasize an important continuity between the two I have dealt with them in the same terms. It is the same procedure Jackson follows when she counts the Marquis de Sade as a fantasy writer, or when she excludes *The Wizard of Oz* while including *Alice in Wonderland*. Subversion is an important, even defining criterion for her. For me, revealing 'the unsaid and unseen of a culture' may not always subvert that culture's assumptions; it may only display them in the fantastic mode.

9 Jackson, 3–4.
10 Jackson, 4.
11 Jameson, 191.
12 Both *Blood Sport* and *Deliverance* emphasize that masculine knowledge is paid for with death or mutilation. In both there is a return to civilization by a figure with an Oedipal limp: Lewis, and the father whose poisoned foot has had to be amputated. The principle these men have pursued can kill, but is itself unkillable; a man cannot really win against it, only yield to it.

There is also the constant possibility of self-delusion – as Mailer would understand so well – in the midst of the very actions by which a man is proving himself. See, for instance, Peter G. Beidler's article, ' "The Pride of Thine Heart Hath Deceived Thee": Narrative Distortion in Dickey's *Deliverance*', *South Carolina Review* 5, i: 29–40. Beidler sees the one 'that dwelleth in the clefts of the rock' to be Ed Gentry, midway up the cliff he scales. He traces various ways in which that cliff-dweller could be deceiving himself, as the book's epigraph indicates, to the point of killing an innocent man. It is too much to say that this is the whole point of the book, but Dickey has included details that cast doubt on the rightness of Ed's actions, even in Ed's own mind. This doubt is another kind of trial of one's masculine ability to judge and act.
13 Jackson, 35.
14 Norman Mailer, *Existential Errands* (Boston: Little, Brown, 1963), 90–1.

7 Supermale

1 E. Nelson Bridwell, *Superman: From the 30's to the 70's* (New York: Bonanza, 1971), 8.
2 Joseph Campbell, *The Masks of God*, III (New York: Viking Press, 1959–1968).
3 Jacques-Henry Levesque, *Alfred Jarry* (Paris: Seghers, 1973), 33.
4 Alfred Jarry, *Oeuvres Completes IV* (Geneve: Slatkine Reprints, 1975), 228.
5 Roger Shattuck, *The Banquet Years* (London: Faber & Faber, 1959), 166.
6 Alfred Jarry, *The Supermale*, trans. Ralph Gladstone and Barbara Wright (New York: New Directions, 1977). Citations to this edition will be given in the text.
7 Jarry, *Oeuvres Completes* I, 74.
8 Jarry, *Oeuvres Completes* III, 22.
9 George Bernard Shaw, *Complete Plays with Prefaces*, III (New York: Dodd, Mead & Co., 1963), 488, 492.
10 Shattuck, 164–5.
11 Shattuck, 168.
12 Jarry, *Oeuvres Completes* VII, 137.
13 Philip Jose Farmer, *A Feast Unknown* (North Hollywood, Calif.: Essex House, 1969).

8 The terrain of truth

1 Michel Leiris, *Miroir de la tauromachie* (Paris: GLM, 1964), 30. All translations from this work are my own.
2 Leiris, *Miroir*, 30–1.
3 Michel Leiris, *Manhood*, tr. Richard Howard (New York: Grossman, 1963), 152.
4 Leiris, *Manhood*, 160.
5 Leiris, *Manhood*, 158–9.
6 Leiris, *Manhood*, 159.
7 Leiris, *Manhood*, 157.
8 Leiris, *Miroir*, 46.
9 Leiris, *Manhood*, 93.
10 Jeffrey Mehlman. *A Structural Study of Autobiography: Proust, Leiris, Sartre, Levi-Strauss* (Ithaca, N.Y.: Cornell University Press, 1974), 80–1.
11 Leiris, *Manhood*, 89.
12 Leiris, *Miroir*, 42.
13 Leiris, *Miroir*, 22.
14 *Phoenix II: Uncollected, Unpublished and Other Prose Works by D.H. Lawrence*, ed. Warren Roberts and Harry T. Moore (New York: Viking, 1968), 276.
15 Leiris, *Miroir*, 43.
16 Leiris, *Manhood*, 156.
17 George Steiner, *After Babel: Aspects of Language and Translation* (New York: Oxford U. Press, 1975), 39.
18 Leiris, *Manhood*, 56.
19 Philip Roth, *My Life as a Man* (New York: Holt, Rinehart & Winston, 1974), 100. Page citations to this work will be given in the text.
20 Leiris, *Manhood*, 161–2.
21 Jose Ortega y Gasset, 'Notes on the Novel', in *The Dehumanization of Art* (New York: Doubleday, 1956).
22 Leiris, *Manhood*, 105.
23 Doris Lessing, *The Golden Notebook* (New York: Simon & Schuster, 1962), xii.
24 I have borrowed the term from Erik Erikson, of course – though without Erikson's assumption that because of its connections with the womb, a woman's 'inner space' is best fulfilled by child-bearing. Kate Millett exposes the fallacy of this in her *Sexual Politics* (New York: Doubleday, 1970), 210–20.
25 Leiris, *Manhood*, 151.

INDEX

Aldridge, John, 27
Anderson, Sherwood, 155
Appignanensi, Lisa, 10–11
authenticity, 136–7
autobiography, 136–7, 138–40,
   142–3, 147

bullfight, the, 36; Hemingway
   and, 133; imagery of, 133, 136–7;
   Miroir de la tauromachie, 133–4;
   sexual imagery and, 138–9
Burroughs, William, 32

Campbell, Joseph, 103, 119
Cixous, Hélène, 19
Cleland, John, 135–6
Compton-Burnett, Ivy, 5
critics, 1; feminist cs, 1, 6, 18–19,
   156; on Hemingway, 36–8;
   phallic cs, 1
cummings, e.e., 19–20

dandy, the, 128–30
death, 108, 124, 153, 154; Jarry
   and, 124; Leiris and suicide,
   152–3; Mishima and, 51–2, 60–1,
   62, 69–70; reincarnation, 67–8
Derrida, Jacques, 49, 137
Dickey, James, 13; character of Ed
   Gentry, 98–102, 106–9, 116;
   Deliverance, 98–103, 113, 114,
   165n., 166n.; imagery of, 101,
   116; masculinity and, 101–3;
   nature of the body, 106

Don Juan, 127–8
Donovan, Josephine, 32

Eastman, Max, 36–7
Eliot, George, 5–6, 11
epiphanies, 21
Erikson, Erik, 2
Exley, Frederick, 13, 14

fantasy, 113, 116–17
Farmer, Philip José, 131–2
Faulkner, William, 97, 104
feminists, 1, 18–19
Ferreri, Marco, 72
freedom, 108
Freud, Sigmund, 91, 96, 164n.

Galsworthy, John, 9
'gap', the, 137, 138, 140, 145–6,
   147–8, 149–53
Gass, William, 75–6
Gasset, Ortega y, 100–1
Gide, André, 129
Graves, Robert, 76
Greece, 77–8, 80–1
grotesque, the, 78–80, 155

Harrison, Jim, 13
Heller, Joseph, 32
Hemingway, Ernest, 13, 14; 'The
   Battler', 45; 'Big Two-Hearted
   River', 46–8; bullfight and, 133;
   concern with truth, 48–50; *Death
   in the Afternoon*, 36; early stories

Hemingway, contd.
  by, 38–40; 'The End of
  Something', 45; 'erectile
  writing', 75; *A Farewell to Arms*,
  21; *In Our Time*, 40–50; 'Indian
  Camp', 40–3, 45, 48–9; limits of
  male values, 45; masculine
  reserve, 43–50; masculinity of,
  37–8; Max Eastman and, 36–7;
  'The Short Happy Life of Francis
  Macomber', 98; 'Soldier's
  Home', 44–5; 'The Three-Day
  Blow', 45–6; 'A Way You'll
  Never Be', 46; writing style of,
  37–40, 49–50
Hiatt, Mary, 12
homosexuality, 54, 105, 120
Hopkins, Gerard Manley, 8
human body, 71; in *Deliverance*,
  106–8; importance of body to
  Mishima, 59, 62–3, 64;
  relationship between words and
  body, 62–6
hunt, the, 97; *Blood Sport*, 109–13;
  Deliverance, 99–103; h. as
  initiation, 98; lessons learnt
  from, 108–9; 'The Old People',
  97, 103; 'The Short Happy Life of
  Francis Macomber', 98; *Why Are
  We in Vietnam?*, 103–6

imagery: i. of Dickey, 101, 116; i. of
  Hemingway, 42; i. of
  self-petrification, 138; metaphor
  of the bullfight, 133; sexual
  imagery, 138
'inner space', 152, 167n

Jackson, Rosemary, 113, 165n.
James, Henry, 11
Jameson, Frédéric, 103, 114
Jarry, Alfred, 13, 119–20; character
  of André Marcueil, 120–1, 122–6;
  death and, 124; Dandyism and,
  128–9; *Haldernablou*, 120;
  homosexuality, 120; influence of
  Nietzsche on, 126–7; man as
  machine, 122; *The Life and*

  *Opinions of Dr Faustroll,
  'Pataphysician'*, 119, 127;
  Messalina, 127; nature of love,
  123–4, 126; phallic symbols, 120;
  sexuality of, 120; style of
  Supermale, 129–30; *The
  Supermale*, 119, 120–6; *Supermale*
  as a myth of masculinity, 122
Jesperson, Otto, 20–1, 23, 24, 159n
jokes, dirty, 90–3, 95, 96, 164n
Jones, Robert F., *Blood Sport*, 98,
  109–13, 114, 115, 116, 165n
Joyce, James, 75

Kipling, Rudyard, 9, 10
Kolodny, Annette, 7
Kroetsch, Robert, 82, 117;
  Badlands, 82; character of Anna
  Dawe, 83; character of Demeter
  Proudfoot, 85, 86–7, 94;
  character of Hazard Lepage, 85,
  86–7, 91–3, 94; character of
  William Dawe, 82–3; dirty jokes,
  90–2, 95, 96; phallic fixation,
  92–4; *The Studhorse Man*, 82, 85,
  89–90, 93–5; style in *Badlands*,
  84–5; style in *The Studhorse Man*,
  85; themes in *The Studhorse Man*,
  88–9

Lacan, Jacques, 19
Lakoff, Robin, 22
language, 14, 18, 114, 159n.;
  correct speech, 23–4; 'language
  of the flesh', 65; language of
  men, 24, 38, 39, 86; obscene
  speech, 22–3, 26–8, 31;
  sex-related, 1, 20–1; slang, 23,
  26, 31, 38; in *The Studhorse Man*,
  86–7
Lawrence, D.H., 72–3, 76, 78,
  138–9
Legman, Gershon, 91
Leiris, Michel, 13, 152–3; 'The
  Autobiographer as Torero', 135,
  136; autobiography and, 138–40;
  hardness and, 138; imagery of
  self-petrification, 138; Jeffrey

Mehlman and, 138; *Manhood*, 135, 139, 140; metaphor of the bullfight, 133; *Miroir de la tauromachie*, 133–4, 137, 145; plenitude and, 137; sexual imagery, 138, 147; views of suicide, 152–3

Lessing, Doris: *The Golden Notebook*, 150–2

macho, 43, 45, 110, 111, 118, 137, 156

Mailer, Norman, 13, 14, 28–9, 46; actions related to writing, 30–1; *Advertisements for Myself*, 17; *An American Dream*, 30, 33, 36; *The Armies of the Night*, 17; bullfight and, 133; *Cannibals and Christians*, 17, 28; *The Executioner's Song*, 21; importance of being tough, 20; influence of Hemingway on, 36; 'The Language of Men', 24–5; masculinity and, 16–17, 31–2, 33, 34–5, 105, 117; mystical element in, 33–4; *The Naked and the Dead*, 33; need for danger, 28, 30, 31; obscenity and, 26–8, 31; *The Prisoner of Sex*, 2, 17, 30, 97; style of, 20, 25–6, 31, 34–5; surrealism, 28–9; 'The Time of her Time', 36; view of women, 17–18; *Why Are We in Vietnam?*, 26–8, 30, 98, 103–6, 112, 114–16; writing and, 18, 20, 29–30, 115

masculinity (manhood), 3, 7–9, 27, 117, 156–7; achieving manhood, 97–8, 109, 145; archetypal manhood, 102, 109; autobiography and, 137; death and, 153; Dickey and, 101–3; distrust of talking, 44–5; female element in, 31; Hemingway and, 37–8; initiation process, 98, 102, 106, 113; Jarry and, 120; Kroetsch and, 82, 88–9; language and, 114; Leiris and, 133; limits of male values, 45,

111; *macho* values, 43, 45, 110, 111, 118; Mailer and, 16–17, 30–2, 34–5, 105, 117; masculine reserve, 43–50, 53; Mishima and, 54, 69–70; 'My Life as Man', 150; myths of m., 112–13, 122, 127–8; 'natural' man, 9; nostalgia, 102–3, 165n; optimism about m., 154; self-consciousness, 8–9, 14, 19, 155, 156, 157; *see also* the hunt

Masson, André, 137

Mead, Margaret, 2–3

Mehlman, Jeffrey, 138

Men's Movement, 7, 154

Miles, Rosalind, 1, 5

Miller, Henry, 28–9

Millett, Kate, 2, 3, 23

Mishima, Yukio, 13, 14, 113, 155; boyhood of, 53–4; character of Honda, 55, 57, 67–9; character of Tōru, 56–7, 67–8; *Confessions of a Mask*, 58–9; death and, 51–2, 60–1, 62, 69–70; death and reincarnation, 67–8; *The Decay of the Angel*, 51, 57; freedom and, 66; homosexuality of, 54; importance of the body to, 59, 62–3, 64; interaction of art and action, 52–3; masculinity and, 54, 69–70; metaphor and, 61–2; objectivity and, 60–2; relationship between words and body, 62–6; relationship with words, 54–5, 62–3, 66–7; *The Sailor Who Fell from Grace with the Sea*, 55; *The Sea of Fertility*, 55–7, 67–9; self-awareness, 55–7, 58, 61; *Sun and Steel*, 57–8, 59–61, 70; theory of beauty, 58–60; voyeurism in, 55

Moravia, Alberto, 13; *The Two of Us*, 73–5, 77, 79–81

Musil, Robert, 11

mysticism, 23–4

Nietzsche, Friedrich, 126–8

Oedipus complex, 110, 111, 112
Oldenburg, Claes, 75

Pater, Walter, 8
penis, 71–2, 81; 'Down, Wanton,
    Down', 76; grotesque and,
    78–81; independence of, 72–3;
    Lady Chatterley's Lover, 72–3;
    Portnoy's Complaint, 73, 77, 79;
    profundity and comicality of,
    76, 77; role in *The Last Woman*,
    72; *The Studhorse Man*, 86, 87–8,
    92; style and, 75–6, 77, 93; *The
    Two of Us*, 73–5, 77, 79–81
phallic critics, 1
phallus, 19, 77–8, 163n.; bull as
    phallic symbol, 133; Jarry's use
    of phallic symbols, 120; Leiris's
    imagery and, 138; phallic
    illustrations in *Miroir de la
    tauromachie*, 137
Piercy, Marge, 18
Playgirl, 71
plenitude, 136–7
Proust, Marcel, 11

Radin, Paul, 93
Richardson, Dorothy, 4, 11
Roth, Philip, 13; *Portnoy's
    Complaint*, 73, 77, 79
Roth, Philip: *My Life as Man*, 141,
    147–8; attitude to the 'gap',
    151–2; character of Maureen,
    145–6; character of Tarnopol,
    141, 143–4, 146–50; Dr
    Spielvogel, 148–9; form of,
    141–3, 148; illusion of reality,
    145; inconsistency in, 144–5;
    preoccupation with
    masculinity, 150; 'self', 141–2;
    shifts in style, 144; woman as
    gap, 146

Sarraute, Nathalie, 5
Schorer, Mark, 37–8
'self', 141–2
self-awareness, 55–7, 58, 61
self-consciousness, 8–10, 12–13,
    14, 19, 155, 156, 157
self-destructiveness, 155
Seneca, 18
sensitivity, 13–14
sex definition, 2–3
Shaw, George Bernard, 1, 126–8
Sheldon, Alice B., 11
Silverberg, Robert, 11
Spacks, Patricia Mayer, 1–2, 3
Steiner, George, 21–2, 139–40
superhero, 118–19, 130–2
Superman, 118, 131

truth, 48–50

Vinci, Leonardo da, 72
Virility School, 13–15, 52, 54, 89,
    133, 154

Walters, Margaret, 71
women, 17–18
Women's Movement, 3–4, 8, 154–5
Woolf, Virginia, 4, 9–11, 12, 13, 14,
    21; *To the Lighthouse*, 5; *A Room of
    One's Own*, 8
writing, 138–40
writing style, 1, 3, 12, 14, 155–6;
    female writers and, 3–6, 9–10;
    feminine style, 11, 12, 156; first
    person narration, 114–15;
    Hemingway's, 37–40, 49–50;
    influenced by the penis, 75–6,
    93; Kroetsch's, 83–4; Mailer's,
    30; 'masculine sentence', 6–7;
    masculine style, 7–8, 13, 14, 85,
    114, 156; Mishima's, 53, 63, 64,
    65; Roth's, 144; 'woman's
    sentence', 3–5, 11